EASTER ISLAND'S SILENT SENTINELS

EASTER ISLAND'S SILENT SENTINELS

The Sculpture and Architecture of Rapa Nui

KENNETH TREISTER,

PATRICIA VARGAS CASANOVA,

AND CLAUDIO CRISTINO

Foreword by DANIEL LIBESKIND

Maps and Illustrations by ROBERTO IZAURIETA *and* KENNETH TREISTER

University of New Mexico Press ⌁ Albuquerque

Photographs by Kenneth Treister, Patricia Vargas Casanova, and Claudio Cristino.
 Additional photographs by Alex Searle and Atariki Cristino.

This publication is made possible in part by a generous contribution from
 Furthermore: a program of the J. M. Kaplan Fund.

Furthermore:
a program of the J. M. Kaplan Fund

LIBRARY OF CONGRESS CATALOGING-IN-PUBLICATION DATA

Treister, Kenneth.
 Easter Island's silent sentinels : the sculpture and architecture of Rapa Nui /
 Kenneth Treister, Patricia Vargas Casanova, and Claudio Cristino ; foreword by
 Daniel Libeskind ; maps and illustrations by Roberto Izaurieta and Kenneth Treister.
    pages cm
 Includes bibliographical references and index.
 ISBN 978-0-8263-5264-4 (cloth : alk. paper) — ISBN 978-0-8263-5266-8 (electronic)
 1. Easter Island—Antiquities. 2. Easter Island—History.
 I. Vargas, Patricia (Vargas Casanova) II. Cristino Ferrando, Claudio. III. Title.
 F3169.T74 2013
 990—dc23
                        2013013728

Book design and composition by Lila Sanchez
Text is Adobe Garamond Pro 11/13.75; Display type is Trajan, Centaur MT

To the memory of Alan Treister, beloved son, architect, and painter, whose world was his art. In addition we would like to dedicate this book to the early Rapa Nui architects and artists for the inspiring spirit and strength behind their stone monuments and wondrous art.

Contents

FOREWORD

"Who's there?"
—William Shakespeare, *Hamlet*

T HE *moai*—the gigantic figures for which Easter Island is renowned—are alive and breathing. Their large, upward-tilting noses inhale through their massive nostrils. Their disciplined horizontal mouths exhale as if they were exorcising an evil spell. On top of their heads a giant "hat" has been placed. Its heavy weight pushes them to the ground, lest they ascend in meditation like astral bodies of hollow men. They were dead inside the quarry at Rano Raraku, but were brought to a secret life, erected by inexplicable compulsion and hallucinatory passion. Death has passed them by. The moai know that their island (despite appearances) is not shrouded in oblivion; unconcealed yet hidden light plays in their empty eye sockets. Neither are these super-creatures products of cold calculations. The volcanic air that envelops them has been heating more than the pedestals on which they have stood for hundreds of years (and the earth is warm even in the winter). Nor are they reverberating with the echoing shrieks and howls of the terrifying violence that ravaged the island in the past. Their distant, somewhat "what-me-worry" stare chills the heart like a piece of inapplicable theory: there does not exist sufficient wealth on the earth's surface to repay this look.

To a casual visitor, the moai seem destined for an ordeal—a futuristic test of endurance. Stranded in space and enslaved by time, each one is a Hamlet, occupying the space between being and not being.

Aligned in a single row, the moai appear ready for execution by nonexistent powers. The idea of their immortality awakens an uncanny feeling in the visitor: what is the end? Legs have been amputated and the remaining torso hewn into a block of stone, dropped from the precipice of reason.

The island is an always unstable ghost of earthly life. Haunted by forgotten events and voices suffocated by history, the ocean itself is not sated with water, nor fire satisfied by vanished wood. Yet the thing that is most bewildering here is the unobstructed absence that defines every angle of this triangular land. The mystical energy engulfing this piece of dust lost in the nowhere cannot be reversed, cannot be halted, cannot be scorned. It is immune to language, superior to books, incomparable. No animistic, religious, or philosophical desire can construct a mental barrier or protective shield against the lurking power of nothingness that threatens fools and wise alike. There is no horizon ever to be found—not even a rumor of its existence to justify anguish—only hindered beauty lost in unsullied wonder.

Wonder permeates the text and images in this fascinating book. The authors present an accurate and authoritative voyage of discovery to many aspects of Easter Island civilization. The book truly enlightens the reader about the development of the island's architecture, art, and culture. The world as our global village presents Easter Island as a cautionary parable—our memento mori—given the careless exploitation of resources, unsustainable growth, and destruction of nature that we are witnessing.

As a consequence, the reader may well consider new strategies for constructive and creative approaches to life, ones that reaffirm human values. The scholarly research that has gone into this concise and brilliant study of Easter Island is bound to awaken the reader to the enigmas of the past that shape the possibilities of the future.

DANIEL LIBESKIND
NEW YORK

Daniel Libeskind is a world-acclaimed architect, artist, and set designer. He created the Jewish Museum, Berlin; the Grand Canal Theater, Dublin; and the Danish Jewish Museum, Copenhagen, among many others. His work has been exhibited in major museums throughout the world. In 2003, he won the competition to be the master plan architect for New York City's Ground Zero World Trade Center Memorial.

PREFACE

THE genesis of this book occurred in 1988 when one of the authors, Kenneth Treister, an architect interested in the study of indigenous cultures, traveled to Santiago, Chile, to lecture at the Institute for the Study of Easter Island at the University of Chile. Here he met Patricia Vargas Casanova and later Claudio Cristino, the coauthors, who head the institute and have dedicated their professional lives to the study of Easter Island. Then in 1991, Treister, with the guidance of Vargas Casanova, photographed the island and created a documentary film, *Silent Sentinels: The Mystery of Easter Island*, for the government of Chile.

This book brings to the general public—and those who are adventurous explorers at heart—the story of an amazing people who created a remarkable civilization with unique creativity in one of the loneliest places in the world. It is about a people conspicuous among ancient civilizations who, in spite of their isolated geography, created a handsome, vernacular architecture and unequaled gigantic stone colossi, all fashioned out of the simplest of building materials, stone.

This book is well illustrated and full of the authors' photography, for the reality of the island's amazing achievements can only be understood visually, by seeing photographs of its extensive archaeological ruins.

In addition to the book's primary focus as a broad, general survey of the history, culture, and art of Easter Island, it has three unique features. First, the conjectural reconstruction by Treister of the prehistoric, thatched pole houses based on ancient postholes found at Anakena Beach by Vargas Casanova and Cristino. Second, the book relates details of the Easter Island Statuary Project—started in 1977 by Cristino and Vargas Casanova, with a University of Chile team—that made a complete inventory of the moai sculptures scattered about the island. The architecture of the *ahu*, the platform for the giant moai, is well presented as a spectacular expression of prehistoric megalithic architecture.

This book's third unique feature is that it describes in some detail the island's stone architecture. This architecture has not been covered often by other books

for it always seems to be hidden in the shadows cast by the giant stone statues. This anonymous and non-pedigreed architecture is remarkable well beyond its geography or history. It has two particularly interesting aspects: First, it is completely married to the site—a perfect example of contextualism—as its architecture blended into and became part of the island's crust. Second, the architecture used pure geometric shapes and forms. What is remarkable is that the builders were incredible architects, engineers, and landscape planners as their work shows evidence of sophisticated knowledge. This made possible the building of ceremonial complexes with their ahu platforms on which they later erected their statues with their topknots in perfect balance—all without structural failures. Their household architecture used location within the territories, patterned geometric shapes, and quality of materials to present the formal expression of hierarchy and rank.

Easter Island is conspicuous among the islands of the Pacific, not only because of its unique isolation and unequaled archaeological remains, but also because of its accomplishments. The other Pacific islands—many larger, more fertile, and far less isolated—did not rise to the artistic height of Easter Island. As an example, this society invented a writing system incised on wooden tablets; built well-proportioned, tactile temple platforms; and used precisely fitted giant stone blocks, cut and polished so tightly together that they became one.

Finally, this book tells the story of a single day, a day when the workers put down their tools and all creation stopped. A day the island fell silent, when spring suddenly turned to late December. This stunning disintegration brought to shambles all that was created and replaced it with civil war, terror, and cannibalism. Sculptures were pulled down, agriculture abandoned, and the terrified people hid in dark caves.

This book studies the history and archaeological ruins of this small group of vigorous and industrious people who had little, if any, outside stimulus. They created a complex culture and high level of civilization, but their success may have carried within it the seeds of its own destruction. We then ask the question: is the sudden collapse of one of the most isolated laboratories of human achievement a harbinger of things to come to our contemporary, spinning-ever-more-wildly world, or is it just another anecdotal story in the long history of humankind?

Rano Raraku quarry with statues on the southwest slope.

Ahu Nau Nau, now restored. Once bonfires blazed at each statue.

INTRODUCTION

The nearest solid land the islanders can see is above, in the firmament, the moon and the planets.
Living nearest the stars, they know more names of stars than of towns and countries in our own world.

—Thor Heyerdahl, *Aku-Aku, The Secret of Easter Island*, 1958

IN the midst of the world's greatest ocean, in a region seldom traveled, lies a lonely, mysterious island. It has no neighbors; in every direction looms a vast and threatening void. At night the heavens above this island truly sparkle. No veil of city lights dulls the spectacle or deprives the senses. The sensation is one of untold peace. By day, the experience is no less poignant—the blue bowl of sky lightly resting on the mirror sea, with man hugging a humble rock in the midst of it all. Inland the island is deathly quiet, except on the wind-swept heights or along the shore where the crashing surf intrudes relentlessly on the ear.

And then there are the statues. Less than three centuries ago, the first explorers observed the island natives squatting before mammoth stone images, prayerfully raising and lowering their arms with palms pressed together. Bonfires blazed at the foot of the statues. The next morning the islanders lay face down along the shore, worshipping the statues as the sun rose, with hundreds of fires lit all around. Today most of the statues stand no more. They lie prostrate, toppled from their stands in a blood-thirsty spree of destruction.

In the study of great civilizations, we find many that are grand in both their history and influence. But few excite the imagination, elicit as much astonishment, and exude as much mystery as does this desolate volcanic speck. First encountered by the Dutch during Jacob Roggeveen's expedition, it was named for its day of discovery, Easter Sunday, April 5, 1722.

Imagine a sixty-three square-mile (163.6 square-kilometer or 40,426-acre) volcanic rock surrounded by a million square miles of deserted ocean, almost fourteen hundred miles from the coast of South America (1,361 miles to southern Chile or 1,467 miles along latitude 27°). In this loneliest spot on earth, a people created a complex society; they developed sophisticated astronomic knowledge, exquisite wood sculpture, a comprehensive monumental stone architecture, roads, and a puzzling ideographic script. And then they went about sculpting giant "living faces" in stone. Oral traditions indicate Easter Island's statues (moai) represented their honorable and powerful ancestors. When the spirits of those ancestors entered into the statue—after their eye sockets were carved at the ceremonial platform—they became "alive" and were called living faces (*aringa ora*).

Easter Island is shrouded in mystery: Who were the first inhabitants, and how did they come to settle on the tiny, grass-covered island described by the eighteenth-century European visitors? How was it they not only survived but went on to create magnificent art and architecture in a rocky place, almost completely cut off from any other people for several centuries? How did they develop the basic principles of sound architectural design, the use of pure geometry, symmetry, and meaningful standardized patterns of spatial relationships? What motivated them to carve, transport, and erect their giant stone statues, some weighing as much as one hundred metric tons? Why did they topple these statues, in a series of mutually destructive wars, destroying centuries of human effort?

Easter Island's sophistication in the creation of their stone architecture and sculpture is unusual. It was more than a combination of traditions brought from other places and then their reaction to the problems of their environment. In this case, they added new, original, and creative elements, which gave birth to an aesthetic, rational, and highly patterned architecture perfectly in tune with its environment and its unique, monumental stone sculptures.

Let us explore this mysterious island at the end of

the sea, which experienced a burst of glory unknown to the rest of the world. This wondrous culture gradually became frail and its brilliance withered, collapsed, and faded into oblivion.

Easter Island did not suffer a mind-numbing isolation after colonization. Interaction both to the west and perhaps on occasions to the east was simply less repetitive or continuous than elsewhere in Eastern Polynesia, and Easter Island became effectively isolated circa AD 1600 when contacts with neighboring islands like Mangareva, Pitcairn, and Henderson ceased. Between AD 1600 and the early 1800s Easter Island truly became Te Pito O Te Henua, or "the end of the land." Until the nineteenth century it would remain earth's most isolated inhabited island. The island was more isolated than ever during the late 1800s and mid-1900s.

The island's Golden Age was certainly the fifteenth century, and from then onward it was downhill. They were building a new society out of the ruins when the Europeans arrived early in the eighteenth century.

What lasted are its stone sculptures and the fossil shell of its stone architecture. This architecture, though simple, is beautiful in its simplistic execution and geometry. It silently echoes the remains of a once flourishing society.

It has been said that a great waterfall in the deepest jungle is silent if no one is there to hear it. Is a great civilization any less remarkable when no others are there to observe it? Here then is a glimpse of the stone legacy of a unique people who discovered, settled, and subsequently tamed a completely isolated mote of windswept rock surrounded by an endless sea.

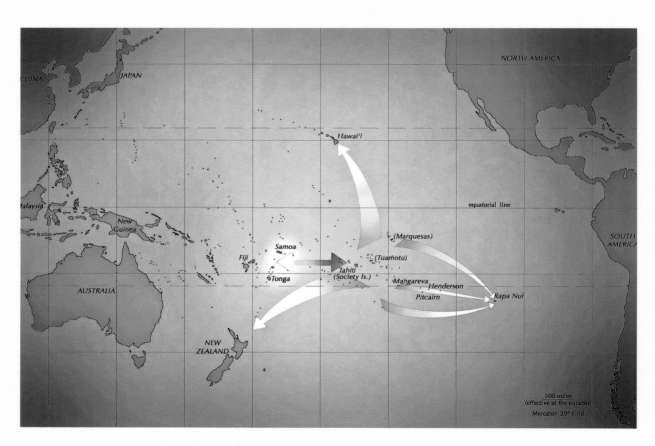

Easter Island (Rapa Nui), an isolated dot in the vast Pacific Ocean. Arrows indicate possible settlement and trade routes. Reproduced from Vargas Casanova, Cristino, and Izaurieta, *1000 Años en Rapa Nui*.

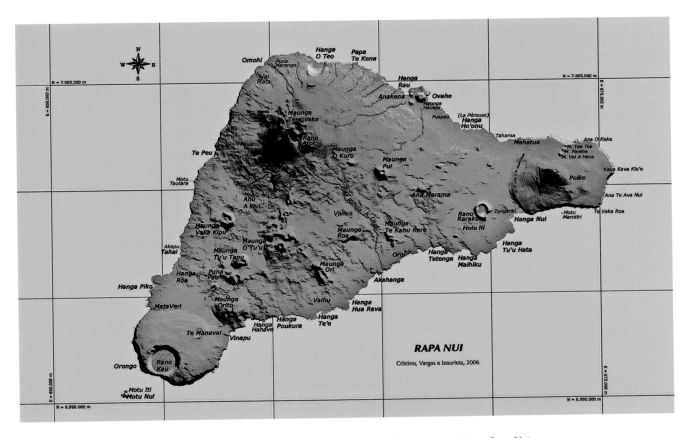

Easter Island with main place names. Reproduced from Vargas Casanova, Cristino, and Izaurieta, *1000 Años en Rapa Nui*.

Chapter 1

A SURREALISTIC GEOGRAPHY

Figure 1.1. Petroglyphs, silhouetted against the Pacific Ocean and carved into the natural stone outcroppings, at the ceremonial village of Orongo.

CIVILIZATIONS throughout history have been strongly influenced by their environments. Some existed in relatively amenable areas of the world where they could easily mold and shape their natural surroundings to meet their needs. Others found themselves in areas of harsh and intractable geography where survival and mere accommodation took precedence in their culture's development.

In studying the architecture of Easter Island, it is essential to understand the severe and almost surrealistic geographical conditions that prevailed a few centuries after the arrival of the first Polynesians. Once understood, it becomes easy to see how appropriate Easter Island's architecture was to this stone island. Not only did Easter Islanders fit and adapt to their island's dominating geology, but they shaped most of their built environment out of their one abundant material, volcanic stone. In addition to the stone architecture, they developed diverse residential architecture in wood and grass and used hundred of caves, formed by the natural crust of the earth, for shelter and protection.

Easter Island, a small volcanic island shaped like a triangle, is located just below the Tropic of Capricorn, 2,360 miles west of the port of Caldera in South America and, its mother country since 1888, Chile. It is the eastern-most Polynesian island.

This triangle was created by the eruption of three large volcanoes, now inactive, that dominate the island. The highest and youngest is Mount Tere Vaka at 1,700 feet, containing a small crater lake named Rano Aroi. The second and oldest, standing at 1,200 feet high with basalt layers dating back three million years, is Poike in the eastern corner of the island. The southwest corner of the island is marked by the imposing cliffs and crater of Rano Kau, lush with green vegetation, containing a mile-wide freshwater lake 390 feet above the sea, which was, in ancient days, the most important reservoir on the island. The southern side by this volcanic crater has been eroded by thousands of years of pounding by the sea, creating a sheer cliff one thousand feet high. Someday it will crumble with a thunderous roar, opening the crater like the bursting

Figure 1.2. Kari Kari, the lowest rim of Rano Kau's crater, with the crater lake on the left and the Pacific Ocean on the right.

Figure 1.3. Rano Kau volcano defines the southwestern corner of the island.

Figure 1.4. Today Easter Island's treeless landscape is composed of rolling hills covered by a wavy carpet of grass.

Figure 1.5. The shallow turquoise waters at Anakena Beach on the north coast. This beautiful horseshoe-shaped bay is thought to be where the first settlers arrived.

Figure 1.6. Rano Raraku volcano in the island's southeast.

of a dam into the sea. This is the site of the sacred village of Orongo, a most exquisite example of stone architecture and village planning.

The island's surface consists of volcanic ash and rock. The land surface is covered with blocks of lava, rocky outcroppings, and sharp-edged stones of all sizes scattered like a crusty blanket on the ground. The soil is in places razor thin and in places thick and fertile. The island's almost treeless landscape is dominated by round hills with gently sloping sides, covered entirely by a waving carpet of grass. Most of these hills are part of the series of about seventy secondary craters and parasitic cones of the main volcanoes that reveal the complex events that shaped the island, two of which played a significant role in the development of the sculptural art of the ancient society. Rano Raraku volcano was the quarry for the giant stone sculptures, and Puna Pau volcano was the quarry where the large, red headdresses for the (moai) statues were cut and fashioned.

The climate is mild, consistent, and subtropical, a weather that originally spawned the typical tropical vegetation that conjures up visions of a Polynesian heaven on earth.

In the path of the trade winds and battered by strong local winds there are no deep and protected harbors or crescent coastal lagoons that would have allowed greater use of the sea. The exposed seacoast has been shaped by erosion, severely undercut by the roaring surf. The rugged basaltic stone, sculpted over millennia into a moonscape, is both fearsome and strangely beautiful. The black, jagged forms appear even stronger and more grotesque when silhouetted against the pure white foam of the sea as it crashes in from its boundless expanse. The entire scene, set to the music of the rolling waves, creates a total work of kinetic art. The snarled volcanic rock towering above the pounding surf is the perfect backdrop for the island's organic architecture and towering sculpture.

Let's compare Easter Island with the typical tropical high-volcanic islands to the west. This forbidding land lacks the most typical Polynesian amenities—the coral reefs and the long, wide stretches of black volcanic or white sand beaches—which gave their inhabitants

Figure 1.7. The Pacific Ocean beats against the rocky northern coast. The southwestern corner of the island can be seen in the background.

Figure 1.8. The large face of Vai a Heva at Poike volcano with its open mouth carved as a water reservoir.

enjoyment and a place from which to enter and exit the sea. There are but a few tiny beaches on Easter Island. The best is at Anakena Beach—only two hundred feet wide—and the place where oral tradition says the colonizing party led by the mythical founder of the culture, the *ariki* (chief) Hotu Matu'a, first landed a thousand years ago. Covered with rich vegetation and crossed by a perennial stream for centuries, it became the sacred abode of the paramount chiefs of the island.

There are no romantic, nurturing rivers to further man's trade, communication, and quality of life—only a porous volcanic ground that sucked up the rain and, with the exception of the distant crater lakes, left little for man. Once underground, the fresh water flows down to the coast and into the ocean at low tide. Ancient Easter Islanders built trenches and wells to catch the water before it mixed with the sea's saltwater. These water sites became focal points for the ancient settlements and were closely associated with their large ceremonial sites.

Shallow stone reservoirs were used to catch rainwater or spring water inland. Some of these reservoirs were hewn directly in large flat lava beds, while others were sculpted with large carved faces on stone outcrops, like the famous site of Vai A Heva at the Poike volcano (see figure 1.8).

For thousands of years before humans arrived, the island was covered not by desert wasteland but by a subtropical forest, dominated by a large population of cocoid palms. Upon the arrival of man toward the end of the first millennium of the Christian era, in about AD 800–900, the rich volcanic grounds were covered by varied and dense vegetation. Springs, possibly large permanent watercourses, and important endemic fauna, represented mainly by land birds and the most extraordinary variety and number of sea birds in Polynesia, were notable components of Easter Island's landscape.

The AD 800–900 colonization dates proposal came from excavations at Anakena by Arne Skjølsvold et al.[1] in the late 1980s and mainly from our (Vargas Casanova and Cristino) dig there in 1991 with David W. Steadman.[2] However, when colonization took place has been the subject of intense debate since Terry Hunt and Carl Lipo, based on their excavations at the sand dunes of Anakena, argued for a later arrival around AD 1250.[3]

In a 2008 article, Marshall I. Weisler (University of Queensland) and Roger C. Green (University of Auckland) clarify the dates for the colonization of Easter Island:

> While we could argue about the merits of their review and rejection of some of the oldest radiocarbon dates for Rapa Nui, what is less controversial is the current dating for Mangareva and the Pitcairn Group and the related claim of its compatibility with a date of 1200 CE for Rapa Nui. These islands are, on all evidence to date, the source of the founding population for Rapa Nui based on geographic position, radiocarbon dates, linguistics, material culture, introduced flora and fauna, physical anthropology, and voyaging feasibility.
>
> Based on our brief review of colonization dates for Mangareva and the Pitcairn Group below, we disagree with Hunt and Lipo that "a date of about AD 1200 for the colonization of Rapa Nui *fits well with the evidence that has emerged for colonization from elsewhere in the southeastern Pacific*." (2006:1605, *emphasis the authors*). Our review also underscores the need to examine colonization dates at the regional level, (Weisler, 1998) especially when it relates to the probable source of colonists that founded Rapa Nui.
>
> Even one of the strong supporters for a generally late colonization scenario throughout East Polynesia cites the earliest known settlement of Anakena as dating to 1000 CE (Anderson 2006:275). This assessment is fully compatible with that of Vargas Casanova et al. (2006:403), who find there is no data from Rapa Nui at present to sustain an initial settlement more ancient than 800 CE nor for one judged to be later than 1000 CE. They base their evaluation on a detailed examination of their 1991 excavations at Anakena and the fine detail of its stratigraphic record, radiocarbon age determinations, fauna, cultural artifacts, their reinvestigations of the Poike "Ditch" feature, and their more general overview of all other well-dated sites investigated by others on that island.[4]

Patrick V. Kirch (University of California, Berkeley), who has conducted extensive archaeological and ethnoecological research throughout the Pacific Islands over the past three decades, thoroughly reviews multidisciplinary advances in knowledge and presents a chronology of the Pacific Islands' settlement, including possible connections to South America in a recent article:

> The human colonization of the Pacific is an enduring problem in historical anthropology. Recent advances in archaeology, historical linguistics, and bio anthropology have coalesced to form a set of models for population movements and interactions in Oceania, which have been tested on independent data sets. Earliest human movements into Near Oceania began about 40,000 years ago, resulting in great cultural, linguistic, and genetic diversity in this region. About 4,000 years ago, the expansion of Austronesian speakers out of Southeast Asia led to the emergence of the Lapita cultural complex in Near Oceania. The Lapita expansion into Remote Oceania, commencing about 1200 BC, led ultimately to the settlement of the vast eastern Pacific, ending with the colonization of New Zealand about AD 1250. Polynesians probably reached the coast of South America, returning with the sweet potato and possibly the bottle gourd. Polynesian influences on New World cultures remain a topic of debate.
>
> The emerging picture is one of a fairly rapid Polynesian colonization of the chain of islands stretching from the Australs to Mangareva, Pitcairn-Henderson, and finally to Easter Island that occurred between roughly AD 800 and 1000.[5]

The original settlers found the island covered with thick bush and forests made up predominately of palms. Later, other tree species would be introduced from subsequent Polynesian visitors. The first one hundred to two hundred years of human habitation caused little change to the island's vegetation. Now there are no signs of the original rain forest or verdant jungles and swaying trees that once created motion and lazy shade. The virgin forest was decimated early as man

Figure 1.9. The grass covers the plains today. Different varieties were introduced for livestock feeding.

starting to clear land for agriculture and continued destroying it centuries later with overuse and wartime burning. There are no more deep green valleys or lushly landscaped ravines—just a monotonous, rocky landscape of rolling hills with patches of newly introduced trees above endless grassy plains. The landscape more closely resembles Scotland and other rough, colder lands.

In every way this island became inhospitable after several centuries of human occupation, yet on its increasingly barren shores there blossomed for nearly a thousand years a surprisingly advanced and complex culture. During its late prehistoric period, the period prior to European discovery, the island was highly isolated and bereft of the comfort, knowledge, and nourishment that man derives from contact with his fellow man.

They did, however, find a few ways to conserve precious water for their plants. One method included planting in natural crevices that had formed in the volcanic rock. Later they even drilled holes to further expand this practice. Originally agriculture was conducted on the flat, easy-to-work plains but as more land for crops was needed to support the growing population, they started clearing the land for their plantations by cutting the forest located on the hills moving from the coast toward the interior of the island. Scientific evidence today illustrates "dramatic processes of deforestation, soil erosion and other irreversible changes of the fragile ecosystem of Easter Island and many other islands of Polynesia. Some investigators tie these changes to important regional or global climatic and environmental phenomena while others see them as a direct consequence of the impact—on a previously unsuspected scale—of the arrival of man to the region. The exponential growth of those populations that reached considerable high numbers in a few generations; the over exploitation of natural resources; and the expansion of agriculture among other processes progressively caused radical transformations of these pristine and fragile island ecosystems, often making human occupation untenable."[6]

Indications exist that "in the soil profile of southwest Poike, planting pits characterize the yellowish brownish soil, too, this also being evidence of agricultural land use. The garden pits contain fertile soil with a loose structure. Charcoal is often enriched in the pits

as it was used as fertilizer. Since the palm root channels have not been destroyed by agricultural practices, the palm trees must have existed while agriculture was carried out between the palms."[7]

By the time the Western explorers discovered Easter Island, during a period when the natives were trying to rebuild their culture after a period of decline and near collapse, most of the large forests had been destroyed. The most common observation of the eighteenth-century European expeditions led by Roggeveen, González, Cook, and La Pérouse was the scarcity and progressive disappearance of large trees. In 1774, J. R. Forster found this was remarkable "on an isle of this extent, under so fine a climate and inhabited for a long time past."[8]

By the early twentieth century only about thirty flowering plants, fourteen ferns, and fourteen mosses are considered to be indigenous. "There is in the Pacific Ocean no island of the size, geology, and altitude of Easter Island with such an extremely poor flora and with a subtropical climate favorable for plant growth, nor is there an island as isolated as this, and the conclusion will be that poverty is the result of isolation—even if man is responsible for the disappearance of part of the flora, it cannot have been rich," said the early naturalist and explorer Dr. Carl Skottsberg.[9]

The denuded contemporary landscape, with extensive prairies first described by some of the early visitors, was the result of three things: slash and burn agriculture practiced on a great scale by the prehistoric Polynesians; complex cultural and environmental changes; and the subsequent historic over exploitation and transformation of this island into a sheep estate. At its apogee in the first half of the twentieth century, stone fences crisscrossed the island, enclosing over seventy thousand sheep. These herds took care of the last relics of native vegetation that are now gone forever. Though the sheep are gone, the stone fences remain.

This ancient culture prized wood. The mythical ariki Hotu Matu'a, head of the initial migration, was gleaned from legend to have introduced species of flora, including several types of trees. These, along with the native trees, were used to make pole houses, construction frameworks, canoes, oars, small utensils, wood sculptures, ornaments, and large logs used to build scaffolding, levers, rollers, and road tracks for transporting their moai statues from the Rano Raraku quarry to the great megalithic ceremonial altars (ahu) constructed along the coasts of the island. Unfortunately, as the need for wood grew with an increasing population, the propagation of trees did not keep up with the demand, and the wood supply was eventually exhausted. The lack of logs large enough to transport the island's huge statues puzzled the first European explorers and generations of researchers before the advent of the scientific study of pollen, grains, and other spores, which unlocked the prehistoric past.

As the forest was decimated by man, wood became scarce and highly valued by the natives. Driftwood became highly prized and was used to carve their most precious ornaments and small sculptures, like the kava-kava figurines, and eventually it was also used to carve some of the invaluable incised hieroglyphics on their *rongo-rongo* boards that contained their puzzling symbolic script.

According to Christopher M. Stevenson, an archaeologist at the Virginia Department of Historic Resources, "The ancient Rapanui people did abuse their environment, but they were also developing sustainable practices—innovating, experimenting, trying to adapt to a risky environment—and they would still be here in traditional form if it were not for the diseases introduced by European settlers in the 1800s. Societies don't just go into a tailspin and self-destruct," says Stevenson. "They can and do adapt, and they emerge in new ways. The key is to put more back into the system than is taken out."

While evidence suggests the Rapanui people cut down or destroyed about six million trees in three hundred years as a consequence of slash and burn agriculture, for example, they were also developing new technological and agricultural practices along the way—such as fertilization techniques to restore the health of the soil and rock gardens to protect the plants.

Other archaeological evidence indicates that the Rapanui people radically changed their societal structure from one dominated by chiefs to one that was much more egalitarian in nature, which effectively leveled out their consumption patterns.

Water for agriculture, limited due to deforestation and other natural phenomena, dictated adopting methods of water conservation. Joan A. Wozniak described what she found in the environs of Ahu Te Niu in the northwest coastal region as garden areas where the islanders used the natural layers found in the volcanic crust of the island to plant crops between those layers, so as to save water and create shade for the plants to keep down evaporation. Here the islanders used the natural terrain in a creative way: "Several excavations indicated the presence of garden areas. These garden areas tend to have a layer of lithic mulch over a silty loam layer with pit features containing charcoal, obsidian, and other imported materials. Ethnographic and archaeological evidence indicates that the rocks were used to control humidity within garden areas."[10]

Accounts of early visitors varied as to the quality of the soil and the fertility of the ground, but it appears that the island had extensive plantations of sweet potatoes, yams, sugarcane, gourds, paper mulberry, and bananas in prehistoric and early historic times. Descriptions of the plantations by some of the eighteenth-century explorers led many observers to believe that the island was capable of supporting a large population. According to Alfred Métraux, such plantations could have supported three to four thousand natives.

The size of the ancient population of Easter Island is a matter of controversy. Eighteenth century estimates of the population by early observers, who saw and counted the natives near their anchorage or on their expeditions ashore, varied greatly. Their estimates range from about two thousand to eight thousand but are highly unreliable. The official log of Admiral M. Jacob Roggeveen, the Dutch explorer, refers to "the great number of natives," and also makes reference to the majority presence of men. Some European visitors suggest a ratio of five men to one woman. However, the lack of children and women among the natives sighted might be attributed to the islander's fear of foreigners and local intertribal warfare, and the subsequent hiding of large segments of the population in the highlands of the interior or in underground refuge caves. These caves were neatly concealed with walls, passages, and secret entrances after the dramatic consequences of either the initial contacts with Europeans or episodes of intertribal wars.[11]

The language of this ancient culture was recognized, as early as Captain Cook's expedition in 1774, as being closely related to other Polynesian languages, in particular to the speech of Mangareva. One word that probably never existed, however, was a name for the island itself, for some believe that since the island was the entire universe to the natives, they never had a need to name it. Some observers have recorded fragments of the ancient creation myths that lingered in the minds of a few and with them the name Te Pito O Te Henua—the end of the land—to accurately express the extreme geographical isolation of the easternmost island settled by the Polynesians.

Figure 1.10. The denuded contemporary Easter Island landscape of endless grassy plains, with only a few patches of contemporary, introduced trees.

Chapter 2

A TORTURED HISTORY

Figure 2.1. Ahu Akivi, an inland ceremonial platform, with its seven statues, restored by William Mulloy in 1960.

THE settlement of Easter Island in prehistoric times (referring to the time before the discovery of Easter Island by the Dutch in 1722) was by a single culture of Polynesian origin, arriving probably from the Mangareva, Pitcairn, and Henderson islands region, around AD 800 to 900. When the first settlers landed, they found a relatively fertile island, with flat, rocky plains and a park-like savannah and forest covering the hillsides. The initial two hundred years or so of settlement embraced a period of acclimation when the population multiplied rapidly, creating a complex culture that eventually encompassed the entire island.

They developed into a stratified society based on patrilineal descent from their first king, Hotu Matu'a. They organized into large kinship groups, each with a different territory. Their territories extended from the coast into the center of the island where, in some places, a common, neutral area existed. Most of the fresh water sources lay along the coast and around these developed the clan villages, centering on a large communal plaza, the focus of their architectural development.

The early population grew rapidly. Driven by pride and competition among the kinship groups, their world revolved around the representation of their ancestors in monumental stone sculptures. Even though resources were scarce and the ecology delicate, the early population grew rapidly. The Golden Age of Easter Island was a glorious moment in the ancient history of man. It was built without metal, the wheel, or beasts of burden. During this age a holistic and vibrant society was formed. They developed exquisitely fitted masonry walls of cyclopean blocks as well as corbelled stone vaults. They produced a stable agriculture, carved hundreds of stone statues, and constructed long roads to transport them from one single quarry to the ceremonial sites along the coast. During this Golden Age, the island must have been a beehive of ideas, creativeness, and industry. Stone architecture was designed using the meager resources found on the island's volcanic terrain. Huge stone statues were erected as part of larger monumental architectural complexes.

Figure 2.2. The ancestral stone monolithic sculptures, the moai, when in place facing the village, would exude a monumental and heroic power over all.

Figure 2.3

carving and building activities, the forest was consumed, the land became unproductive, and the entire system finally ceased to function. At this point, it is possible the workers rebelled against the rulers and the Golden Age came to an end.

INTERTRIBAL WARS

We do know several of the natural and cultural factors that caused the end of the Golden Age, sometime during the late seventeenth century. This period was marked by the abrupt cessation of the island's Herculean creations. The ensuing years of the seventeenth and eighteenth centuries were characterized by fierce intertribal wars, feuds, cultism, and savage cannibalism. Cannibalism was closely associated with these wars but was abandoned for some reason before the introduction of Christianity to the island.[1]

Waging war was the consequence of profound sociopolitical and religious changes. This may have been a pan-island revolution, of the commoners against the elite members of each tribe, triggered by a generalized degradation of the environment, critical increase of population, and a complex set of negative variables that altered the delicate equilibrium of the whole social, political, and religious system and resulted in cultural collapse and the end of the traditional organization. The destruction and toppling of the statues along with important changes in the function of the ceremonial and religious centers occurred probably after AD 1550 and continued well into the post-European explorers' period until the arrival of Christian missionaries in the nineteenth century.

In 1722, members of the Dutch expedition led by Jacob Roggeveen described some ahu (stone platforms) with giant statues standing near his anchorage off the north coast, probably at Hanga Ho'onu. Captain Cook in 1774 and La Pérouse in 1786 gave similar accounts for the north coast and the west coast near Hanga Roa. During the eighteenth and early nineteenth centuries most ahu in other sections of the island looked like ruins and few statues were seen standing on top of the platforms. By the mid-nineteenth century all of the statues (moai) had been thrown down.

The natives' ceremonial and religious centers focused on the ahu, which were low stone structures used as burial vaults or platforms for the departed. Some

Villages were alive with outdoor activities taking place on communal plazas defined by a crescent of beautifully shaped boathouses.

In the late prehistoric period, owing to their almost complete isolation for probably over a century, the people of the island came to believe they were the sole possessors of the planet. According to their legends, the islanders believed they were the earth's last survivors and that the people in the land of their origin had died out.

Ultimately, a larger percentage of the population was involved in the creation of their giant statues, probably at the expense of other productive activities. As more and more people were drawn into the

Figure 2.4. Ahu Nau Nau seen from the seaside.

Figure 2.5. Birdman petroglyphs cover the rock outcrops at the village of Orongo.

ahu also formed the pedestals for the giant stone moai, which were monumental, carved stone statues of the upper torso of usually a male figure with long earlobes and hands meeting in front. The ahu find their direct equivalent in the stone platforms of the marae in other islands of Polynesia. The term "ahu," a name widely applied to such platforms in central and east Polynesia, denotes ceremonial and burial stone structures.

After the collapse of the Golden Age, the most interesting phenomenon was the rise of the military cult of the Birdman (Tangata Manu). Once the unifying influence of sculpting and building was extinguished and ancestor worship through the moai statues died out, the only unifying force that took its place was this Birdman Cult.

It then appears evident that the people who originally celebrated the Bird Cult included in it reverence for the statues. The ancestors of the present inhabitants were, therefore, the makers of the monoliths of Easter Island and the bird worshippers, thus representing how the old religion of the images blended into and survived with the newer cult.

Like the orders of knights in medieval Europe, the Birdman Cult exemplifies a period of social conflict and strife. The entire social system of the island revolved around this cult that was the last of the old order to exist. Its only lasting memory is found at the ruins of the once exquisite stone ceremonial village of Orongo, a unique architectural complex. Nothing similar existed on Easter Island or anywhere in Polynesia.

Orongo is situated in an unsurpassed wind-blown setting. On one side is a mysterious and dark-green crater lake; on the other, the pounding and swirling Pacific coastline, a thousand feet below.

With the small quantity of animals on the island, next to man, birds were the most interesting creatures and they became the subject of the Birdman religious cult, which was closely linked with the greatest god of the island, Make Make. There was also another spiritual force in the life of the Easter Islander, that of Aku-Aku, a personal spirit, a sort of guardian angel of a region or lineage.

Once a year in the spring, the Birdman Cult celebrated an important rite at Orongo, which overlooks three small offshore islands. At that time of year, the sooty tern came to nest on these islands. The ceremony involved a competition among the chieftains to procure the first egg of the season, which brought back the *mana*—the power of the gods—to the island, and the subsequent installation of the victor as Birdman of the year.[2] The occasion was one of great festivity, for the title of Birdman brought its holder and members of his lineage great power, prestige, and material gain.

Each of the chiefs was represented in the egg hunt by a champion. With the aid of reed floats, the champions would swim, carrying provisions, over a mile to Motu Nui, the largest of the three offshore islands, and camp there, waiting for the birds. The winner was the champion who got the first egg, then swam back to the island, bearing the egg in a small basket tied to his forehead. At that time, the Birdman—the tribal chief whose champion had won—shaved his head, brows, and lashes in preparation for the festivities. Then he went down to Mataveri and from there was led in procession to a boathouse (*hare paenga*) located on the southwest exterior slope of the Rano Raraku volcano where he remained in seclusion for one year.[3]

Through the Birdman cult, the warriors managed to surpass the traditional authority of the ariki. Not only did they obtain political power but they acquired an eminent religious position, generating a new sociopolitical organization that was maintained into the historic period.[4]

Figures 2.6, 2.7. Motu Kao Kao, Motu Iti, and Motu Nui, the largest of the three offshore islets, as seen from Mata Ngarau at the ceremonial village of Orongo where the egg hunt of the Birdman festivities took place.

THE PERIOD OF DISCOVERY

Ending the island's long exile from the rest of the world, a period of discovery started when Dutch Admiral Mynheer Jacob Roggeveen made landfall on Easter Day, 1722, while searching for the mysterious Davis Island. He christened his discovery Easter Island, starting a long series of European explorations. After the Dutch, almost fifty years elapsed and then, within a period of sixteen years, the island was visited by Spanish (1770), English (1774), and French (1786) expeditions. The most famous explorer was Captain Cook, who, in 1777, published an account of the island in *A Voyage Towards the South Pole and Round the World*.

THE FINAL DESTRUCTION OF A PEOPLE

Prehistoric population estimates based on archaeological data and back-projections of nineteenth-century historic records suggest that the population of Easter Island reached a peak of over 15,000 people at least one hundred years before the arrival of the Europeans in 1722.[5] By the late 1870s and as the consequence of introduced diseases, slave raids by "blackbirding" (the recruitment of slaves through trickery and kidnappings), and forced emigration to Mangareva and Tahiti, the population plunged to a minimum of between 111 and 140 in 1877. In the late 1800s, thousands of Pacific Islanders and possibly over 2,000 Easter Islanders were removed from their homelands, locked in boats, and carted to Peru to serve as a labor force in the haciendas of northern Peru or the large houses in Lima. Contrary to many sources, there are no records that Polynesians were ever sent to the Chincha Islands, called also the "Guano Islands," off the coast of Peru.[6]

The exploitation of guano (seabird excrement used as fertilizer) on the Chincha Islands off the coast of Peru was a prosperous business in the mid-nineteenth century, and one always short of laborers. That was also the case with the large haciendas. As the number of available slaves became more and more scarce, starting in 1859, slave hunters from Peru made several trips to Oceania to capture natives and sell them into slavery. Though these pirates operated throughout Oceania in their quest for slaves and thousands of natives were kidnapped and removed from their homelands, it seems that the worst consequences fell on the people of Easter Island.

The most egregious of these expeditions between the years 1862 and 1864 had catastrophic consequences for Easter Island and its people. These kidnappers took approximately 2,500 natives, including the king and his son and most of the learned men who could have continued the knowledge of the past civilization.

As Métraux relates, the few who survived the raids were so disheartened that they hid themselves in their caves, lived in great anxiety, and neglected the cultivation of their fields.

Of the thousands of natives enslaved to work on Peru, tuberculosis, smallpox, harsh living and working conditions, bad climate, and unsuitable food killed the great majority. Because of international pressures, particularly from the French and English, 300 or so survivors were put on a ship, many of them with smallpox and tuberculosis, and returned to their homeland. Only 16 arrived alive. This caused an epidemic, further decimating the island's population.[7]

Much of what we know about ancient civilizations is based on oral history. The tragedy of Easter Island is that when thousands were kidnapped during the slave raids, and subsequently ravaged by disease on their return, most oral history died. The only people left to perpetuate it were some of the elderly and small children. Thus, the thread of history—already thin at that point—was drawn even thinner. All the traditions that had persisted for so many years died.

Despite this tragedy, however, cultural historians culled what they could from oral testimony and have been able to piece together the island's legends and history from what few accounts have been handed down over hundreds of years. By taking note of similarities in accounts, one can reconstruct a fairly reliable body of information on the island's history.

THE MISSIONARIES ARRIVE

A period of Christianization started with the arrival of a single missionary from Valparaiso. "Three of the community left for Easter Island, their route taking them by way of Tahiti. Finally, only one continued, Eugene Eyraud, who landed on the island in January 1864." However, with the arrival of only three other missionaries from Chile, by 1868 a rapid conversion to Christianity of the Easter Islanders had occurred. First, their children, a few adults, and eventually the entire society were converted. The missionaries also taught arts and crafts and introduced new foods, cattle, sheep, and other animals to the island.[8]

AN ISLAND OF SHEEP

In 1886 these missionaries brought with them sheep, pigs, horses, cattle, donkeys, cats, rabbits, and pigeons, all of which made a profound impression on the inhabitants of the island where the rat was the only mammal and the chicken was the only domesticated animal. An earlier attempt to introduce mammals (in much smaller numbers) had resulted in the islanders eating them before they had time to multiply. In 1888, Easter Island and the islanders were annexed to Chile. After the tragic revolution of 1891, the Chilean government was unable to continue their initial plans for development in this new territory and, in 1897, Chile leased the entire island to Williamson and Balfour, a British company that turned the island into a grazing ranch for sheep.[9]

Instead of fencing in the sheep, it was easier to fence in the natives, and so they did. The natives were thus relegated to a small section of the island (the small village of Hanga Roa) measuring about eight square miles, while the remainder of the sixty-three square-mile island belonged to the sheep. Except for a handful of company employees, the native population was not allowed to cross the boundaries of their village—Mataveri to the south, Tahai to the north, and Maunga Vaka Kipu to the east—where stone fences defined the line between a once proud people and their rugged island. The people were robbed, not only of their land but of their history and culture, in yet another example of man's inhumanity to man.[10]

Figure 2.8. Stone fences remaining from the twentieth century enclosed over 70,000 sheep when the Williamson and Balfour sheep company rented the island.

Chapter 3

SETTLEMENT AND VILLAGE PLANNING

SETTLEMENTS are organic creations that have their moment of birth, evolving life, and ultimate decline. Settlements offer human beings a sense of place, a sense of identity, and an awareness of their culture, their ancestral roots, and their society's spiritual values. The fossil remains of Rapa Nui's prehistoric settlements clearly tell much about the story of its people.

There were three major stages of settlement development: (1) the establishment of initial settlements at the coastal areas and the division of the main island into several territories (AD 800–900 to AD 1000s); (2) the Ahu Moai or expansion phase (AD 1100–1600s), when most of the ceremonial centers were built in the coastal border and increased land use within the tribal territories resulted in larger population clusters in the coastal plains, and when settlements expanded inland toward the highland boundaries; and (3) the late prehistoric period (AD 1700s), which some authors also refer to as a decadent phase, when environmental deterioration and tribal warfare, along with its consequent population decrease, resulted in the progressive abandonment of the inland areas, a process consolidated in early historic times after permanent European settlements occurred in the late AD 1800s.

Oral tradition tells us that as the island's legendary founder of the culture, the paramount chief-priest Hotu Matu'a, lay on his deathbed, he summoned a counsel of chiefs and divided the island into six districts, each under the control of one of his six sons. Yet ten to eighteen patrilineal descent groups or *mata*, usually described inaccurately as "clans" or "tribes," have been recognized in modern times. It is believed that this discrepancy from the legendary account resulted from further subdivisions of the original six kinship divisions. In 1914, Katherine Routledge recorded the approximate distribution of the main historic lineages on a map (see figure 3.1), which has been interpreted as depicting the boundaries of the ancient territories. However, as Routledge indicated, the dividing lines shown on her map are not defined boundaries and would explain why large sections of the land are shown as either unclaimed or uninhabited.[1] This situation was probably the result of dramatic movements of population in the late prehistoric times and the early historic period.

Rapa Nui's prehistoric lineage territories were fan shaped, spreading in an ever-expanding semicircular fashion out from their compact coastal ceremonial sites to their wider inland areas (see figure 3.2). Family units, in repetitive patterns, each had a distinctive spatial placement and their density increased from the coastal to the inland areas.

There were three broad bands or zones in this fan-shaped pattern: (1) the Ceremonial Zone; (2) the Coastal Plains Zone; and (3) the Interior Zone (see figure 3.2). Each zone was identified by its distinct social status, organization, work distribution, household types, and architectural size and quality, all declining in quality as a function of their distance from the coast.[2]

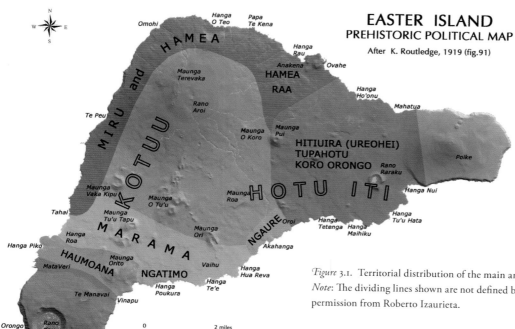

EASTER ISLAND
PREHISTORIC POLITICAL MAP
After K. Routledge, 1919 (fig.91)

Figure 3.1. Territorial distribution of the main ancient mata or patrilineal descent groups. *Note*: The dividing lines shown are not defined boundaries. Illustration reproduced by permission from Roberto Izaurieta.

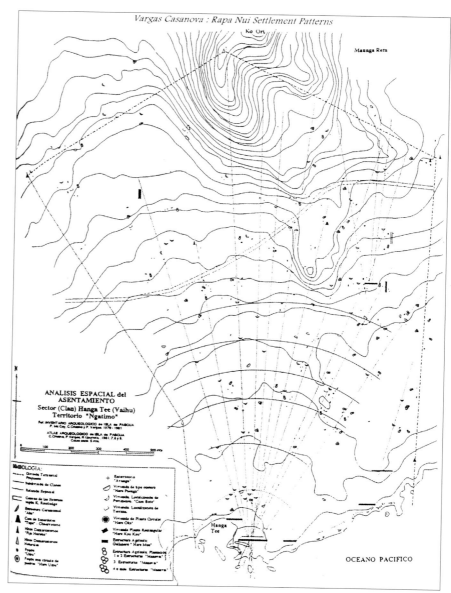

Vargas Casanova : Rapa Nui Settlement Patterns

Figure 3.2. Distribution of architectural components of prehistoric settlement within the Ngatimo mata on the southeast coast. This topographical map shows clearly the small but intense religious and cultural center of the settlement on the coast surrounded by the elite boathouses and then the gradual widening and dispersal of activities as it goes inland. Reproduced by permission from Patricia Vargas Casanova.

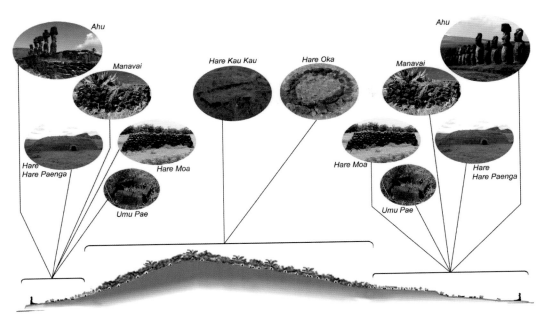

Figure 3.3. Schematic distribution of household types and architectural elements, from the coastal plains to the high inlands.

CEREMONIAL ZONE

The Ceremonial Zone, a monumental outdoor architectural complex, served as the social, political, and religious center of the tribe (mata).[3] This was located in most favorable areas of the coast and was the focus and heart of each mata's territory. This zone consisted of a main monumental altar (ahu) with its visually dominant huge stone sculptures, and a cluster of elaborate elliptical thatched boathouses (hare paenga) facing the ahu and surrounding its unenclosed communal plaza.

The entire village's ceremonial zone—the plaza, the stone image ahu, and their giant stone statues with their backs to the sea and facing the ceremonial plazas—formed one communal environment for daily ceremonies and festivals.

These events held close to the coastal border of the territory were mainly religious practices that enhanced elite social control of the organization of the mata itself. At the edge of the ceremonial complex were the households designed for the tribe's chiefs, priests, and high-status personages. Seaward of the cluster of hare paenga was a sacred area where no domestic activities took place. Here, ancestors, represented by megalithic statues on top of monumental stone platforms, were worshipped, and this is where the cult ceremonies, communal assemblies, investitures, initiations,

redistribution of food, as well as funerary and memorial rituals were held.

The boathouses for the village's elite leaders usually faced the ahu plaza, with the statues and the sea beyond (see figure 3.4). Close by the houses were stone-lined earth ovens (*umu pae*) that were always located in the open and about thirty–eighty feet in front of the houses, at a lower elevation toward the ahu plaza. Archaeological excavations have confirmed that some of these ovens were protected on the windward side with lightly thatched shelters (see figures 4.30a, b and 4.31), while others had shelters built all around to form a kitchen or cook house (*hare umu*). Refuse deposits containing small quantities of fish bones and mollusks suggest some fishing, but collections of these products were scarce. Also, there is no evidence that activities such as fowl husbandry or agriculture occurred here since there were no chicken houses (*hare moa*) or agricultural enclosures (*manavai*) found near the hare paenga cluster in front of the ahu.

Except for ahu, burials, crematories, and hare paenga villages, there were no other constructions in the coastal border reflecting the symbolic significance of this area as a sacred or ceremonial zone linked to their origins and reinforced through ancestral worship. If chicken houses and agricultural enclosures are present in the immediate location of the ahu and villages, these features seem to be from later occupational contexts when the ahu were probably not in use as ceremonial structures anymore. This strongly supports the idea that elite groups inhabiting these households depended upon the redistribution of fowls, horticulture, agriculture, and arboriculture from the commoners' households located inland.

The ruins of several villages are scattered along the entire coast. Some were near creeks and bays where canoes could be landed for fishing. Others were perched on high cliffs but never far from fresh water from springs or wells. The study of some of these ruins indicates that they may have been rebuilt several times.

While the residential complexes associated with the ahu were that of high-ranking members of the society, the rest of the population, the commoners, lived in scattered households further inland in the coastal plains at higher elevations toward the center of the island and close to agricultural fields where they worked.

COASTAL PLAINS ZONE

Inland from the hare paenga cluster and comprising a broader area than the Ceremonial Zone (see figure 3.2), households with horticultural and agricultural features supplied sustenance for themselves and others. There the elliptical floor plans of the commoners' houses were built of a lesser quality and with simpler building materials than in the elites' households. These thatched boathouses were built without stone foundations, their patios were smaller and are found associated with one or more hearths or stone-lined earth ovens (umu pae), agriculture enclosures (manavai), and stone chicken houses (hare moa). These households represented the basic units of the social organization of the extended families, headed probably by the oldest male. Houses built closely together probably constituted family lineages, each one of which apparently had its own ceremonial structures (ahu) within the overall territory of the tribe.[4]

Since it seems the sacred zone was well established early in the historic sequence, it is reasonable that the initial residential settlements would be found in the coastal areas. This indicates most of the surface remains of dwelling sites found in those areas are quite late (AD seventeenth to nineteenth centuries) and suggests that earlier house types other than the boathouse (hare paenga) had been used. These should have been larger pole and thatched structures, possibly of elliptical, circular, or rectangular plan with rounded ends, as indicated by the post-hole patterns (see figures 4.30a, b).[5]

INTERIOR ZONE

Further inland was the Interior Zone, comprising the higher grounds and humid inland areas.[6] Households associated with specialized agricultural practices, arboricultural activities, and lithic workshops were widely dispersed. Altitude and rainfall proved to be the most significant environmental variables with more rain in these higher, interior regions. These complex sites had circular or rectangular houses of lesser size and quality than in the two previous zones, suggesting either a lower status for inhabitants or that they were used on a seasonal basis. The increased use of these uninhabited areas for farming was directly related to the increased population in the other zones.

SUMMARY DISCUSSION

The settlement patterns described in this chapter reflect the underlying principles of the ancient Rapanui social organizational structure. Significant variations in household composition within the territory occupied by a single mata indicate great diversification between each zone. This illustrates not only a highly complex social stratification, "but also substantial differences in functions and specialized activities related to social status, work distribution, and the use of natural resources, and also great variability in agricultural and food production strategies."[7] Thus, the planning of any settlement reflects sharp class distinctions within the boundaries separating the sacred, profane, or domestic activities.

Figure 3.4. The stone foundations and paved patio of the elaborately thatched boathouse (hare paenga) are all that remain. This house, inland from the Ahu Vai Uri at Tahai, opened to its plaza and the statues and was the dwelling of one of the prominent families of the Miru mata tribe on the west coast.

Figures 3.5, 3.6. Off-center on main plazas, there was sometimes a large, circular stone dais. Its function has not been attested to archaeologically, but oral traditions refer to them as used for some kind of memorial ceremonies for notable members of a lineage.

Figure 4.1. Ahu Vai Uri, part of the Tahai ceremonial complex.

Chapter 4

THE ARCHITECTURE OF EASTER ISLAND

In Easter Island the past is the present, it is impossible to escape from it . . . the shadows of the departed builders still possess the land. Voluntary or involuntary the sojourner must hold commune with those old workers; for the whole air vibrates with a vast purpose and energy which has been and is no more.

—Katherine Routledge, *The Mystery of Easter Island*, 1919

Tʜᴇ architecture of Easter Island has been unfairly overshadowed by the island's art, its megalithic statues and stone carvings. While the sculpture may be more extraordinary, the architecture of Easter Island stands as a wonderful example of prehistoric stone construction. In architecture—as in life in general—one appreciates things by comparison. Something looks big in juxtaposition with something small; something high when set against something low. Easter Island's epic stone moai and their related architectural pedestals, which are the subject of so much attention, are monumental and grand especially when compared to the island's early vernacular, domestic architecture, which, though numerous, was simple and indigenous. The national architecture did not stand out, but it demonstrated the islander's admirable talent for blending their structures perfectly into their natural environment.

There are about three hundred monumental, ceremonial, and religious stone ahu in Easter Island that are so visible and prominent that the visitor is seldom aware of the other anthology of building types—the many thousand examples of the island's prehistoric domestic stone architecture—the chicken houses (hare moa); the stone houses found at the Orongo Village; the stone houses known as *tupa*; the stone towers used as land markers (*pipi horeko*); and the stone walled garden enclosures (*manavai*). More numerous during prehistoric times was the domestic wooden architecture of thousands of houses that have now vanished.

Figure 4.2.

Figure 4.3. Informative illustration of a stepped ahu from La Pérouse's 1786 expedition. The statues still have their red-stone topknots and their earlobes have inserted discs for distending the lobes. Notice on the left the fallen topknot. The natives, one on the ahu, one lower left, and possibly one in the top center, are engaged in petty thievery, a common practice noted by the early explorers. Also notice the European mirror being used in the top left. After Heyerdahl, *Archaeology of Easter Island*, 61.

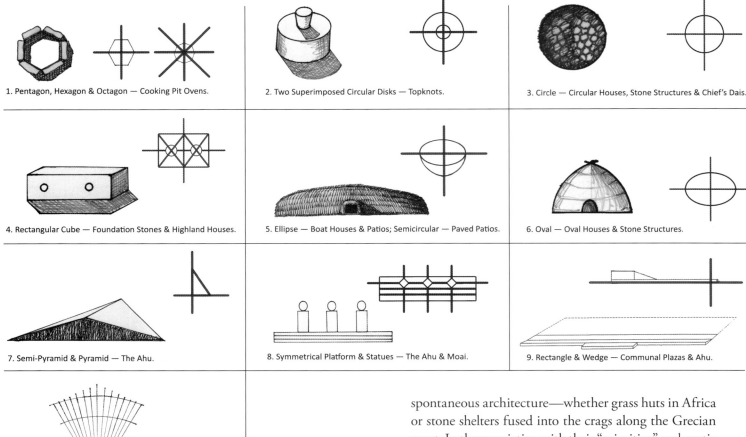

1. Pentagon, Hexagon & Octagon — Cooking Pit Ovens.

2. Two Superimposed Circular Disks — Topknots.

3. Circle — Circular Houses, Stone Structures & Chief's Dais.

4. Rectangular Cube — Foundation Stones & Highland Houses.

5. Ellipse — Boat Houses & Patios; Semicircular — Paved Patios.

6. Oval — Oval Houses & Stone Structures.

7. Semi-Pyramid & Pyramid — The Ahu.

8. Symmetrical Platform & Statues — The Ahu & Moai.

9. Rectangle & Wedge — Communal Plazas & Ahu.

10. Radiating Fan — Coastal Settlement Patterns.

Figure 4.4. Illustration by Kenneth Treister.

These houses can be classified into three distinct types based on their floor plans—elliptical, rectangular, and circular. The record of these houses in the landscape is now almost completely lost. The only remnants we find today are traces of their foundations or perhaps paved patios.

A point of interest about Easter Island's architecture is its geometry and assertiveness on the landscape. It is a strong statement of man's importance in the natural order of things. Most untutored primitive builders with few natural resources start in a basic survival mode and generally build freely with nature. They build informal structures of necessity in a nonpedigreed fashion out of trees and stones; they simply want basic shelter from the rain, the cold, and the wind. Their dwellings welcome the nature around them rather than conquering it—for lack of a generic title it is an anonymous and spontaneous architecture—whether grass huts in Africa or stone shelters fused into the crags along the Grecian coast. In these societies, with their "primitive" and exotic architecture, the line between the natural world and the built environment is blurred.

The Easter Islanders, on the other hand, built with a strong and confident aestheticism—an unusual understanding of the basic principles of design. They built with a mixture of natural, indigenous materials—stones, twigs, dirt, and grass—yet with strong, architectural geometric forms. They appreciated symmetry, order, and three-dimensional solid geometry. Sometimes natural outcroppings of rock were part of their final creation, but these were often altered or modified, again with a strong aesthetic sense.

Their favorite shapes were the ellipse and semi-circle, the geometric forms used in the traditional boat-shaped houses as well as in the stone houses at the ceremonial village of Orongo. They also used the rectangle and circle in the creation of their early thatched houses. In the construction of their ceremonial centers they built the ahu, the islander's monumental stone platforms, with a long inclined plane and symmetrical wings, all opening to a large, well-paved rectangular plaza. This understanding of geometric design seems to have been a spontaneous and continuing architectural custom.

THE AHU

The extraordinary proliferation and variety of monumental architectural forms was perhaps an expression of an effort on the part of the elite to assert their power over the people. Religious and ceremonial architecture became a symbol to the commoner of the elite class's importance and the stability that comes from ancestral roots. Only the elite were direct descendants of the immortalized rulers and knew the traditions and meanings of design.

The ahu have been classified into four distinct types: the image ahu, the semi-pyramid, the *ahu poepoe*, and the rectangular ahu. With the exception of the image ahu, which served the dual function of being the site of funeral ceremonies and supporting the giant statues, all others seemed to have been constructed with only one function: as a burial site. Though a wealth of information exists about these structures, we are not sure of their true sacred function, and knowledge of the ceremonies and other activities held on them remains largely unknown.

Only a few ahu, about 10 percent of the total, were built in the interior highlands; the rest are located along the coast, sometimes two to three hundred feet from the coastal ridge. Some are situated at sea level and some high on the towering coastal cliffs. Of those found on coastal cliffs, a few are large complexes with raised rectangular platforms with or without their architectural appurtenances, such as the symmetrical lower pedestal with its rows of rounded boulders.

The image ahu, or *ahu moai*, were the island's most important architectural monuments. They were not just the platform for the monumental statues but were also conceived as a huge theatrical stage on which the drama of the society was played out. The giant statues, with their sparkling white and red scoria or black obsidian eyes, stood on the ahu giving power and strength to

Figure 4.5. Ahu Ko Te Riku, an image ahu that was part of the Tahai ceremonial complex, at sunset.

the people. They turned their back to the sea and faced their audience—first an elite group of chiefs and priests living in the villages nearby, then the commoners distributed farther inland among the discrete territories of the ancient tribes. No matter where one stood in the village and for some distance beyond, their power was felt; their sight, looking over the people, was highly visible, and their silhouettes were always clear against the bright subtropical sky and the sea beyond.

It is believed the image ahu were sanctuaries that reinforced the distinct lineages of the villager's ancestors. Through several centuries, these ahu evolved from simple stone platforms to very complex and large structures, incorporating numerous architectural, aesthetic, and cult elements. The explorer Katherine Routledge observed in 1914 that these ahu were built in layers over many years, some of rough stone and some of fine.[1]

Some ahu were positioned by astronomical observations. The solstices and equinoxes became, for some observers, the measure for orienting the ahu platform and its surrounding architectural elements. In fact, several ahu seem to have been oriented toward Venus, Mars, or the setting or rising of first-magnitude stars or constellations like Orion and the Pleiades that followed closely the azimuth of the sun and whose rising on June 22 marks the initiation of the ancient Rapanui year. A perpendicular line extended along the long axis of many ahu indicates that they are probably oriented in connection to this event.[2]

Image Ahu

The typical image ahu is a masonry platform or pedestal that held on its top the multiton, monolithic moai carved from volcanic tuff. This type of ahu has a shape that is relatively narrow and elongated. It has a flat top and was constructed of stone walls and slabs, with a core filled with stone rubble.

The image ahu was the masterpiece of Easter Island architecture and the most conspicuous feature of the archaeological landscape. The image ahu is outstanding because of its megalithic sculpture, its fine workmanship, and its strong architectural presence. These structures command an untapped source of inspiration that became beautiful, particularly in relation to the rough and thunderous volcanic coastline and the sea.

The sculptures were considered to be the material

Figure 4.6. Ahu Akivi, an inland ceremonial platform.

objects into which—through offerings, sacrifice, and invocations—the spirits of the ancestors were incarnated, thus the sculptures became aringa ora or "living faces." These stone statues were the symbols of power standing at the edge between the spiritual and material worlds.

The image ahu were altars raised to honor deified ancestors or heads of descent lines, sacred places protected by specific *tapu*. While some belonged to a single extended family and reinforced the distinct lineage from their ancestors, others symbolized the integration of different lineages into a major political unit and were the sociopolitical and religious centers for the different mata (clans).

Their stone pedestals gave the statues added height, increasing the grandeur of the entire architectural composition. The ahu's top platform was often elevated even higher on another wide, secondary platform. Both the upper and the lower platforms had straight walls

running parallel to the sea and, on the inland side—the ahu's important façade—symmetrical masonry wings often spread out on both sides.

The inland side of the secondary platform was in the form of a slightly sloping low ramp paved with beautiful alternating parallel lines of round washed boulders. This ramp was a wonderful architectural statement that created a gradual assent to the ahu and then to the important statue above. This image ahu formed the seaside limit of the village plaza that was artificially leveled and extended inland, flowing into the environs of the elites' village (see figure 4.7). This plaza was often fifty to sixty yards long and there were some that were 120 to 150 yards long. Sections of the plazas were covered with large, flat volcanic rocks laid precisely to create a permanent dark-gray surface of great beauty, particularly when the rocks glistened with sea spray.

The total composition was pure theater: a communal plaza with a stage at its end. The stage had a gradual slope from the plaza to its sets of parallel pedestals, which, in turn, held on high the towering and magical stone statues, their white piercing eyes watching over and mesmerizing all.

These image ahu were architectural monuments that were mostly clustered around a number of coastal centers; their number became less numerous the farther inland one moved. Their workmanship varied considerably. The quality of some architectural structures from the earliest times suggests that the settlers must have arrived on Easter Island with a tradition of excellence in masonry. Examples of fully dressed and fitted masonry are present at the earliest construction phases in Ahu Nau Nau at Anakena on the north coast; in several ahu platforms at Vinapu and Tongariki on the

Figure 4.9. Large and well-adjusted vertical blocks were used for structural stability at the rear wall of the image ahu at Vai Mata.

southeast coast; and at Tepeu and in Ahu Hanga Roa as described by Cook on the west coast.

The masonry of the rear wall (sea side) of some ahu eventually developed to a style of gigantic, precisely fitted vertical basalt blocks, as in Tepeu and Ahu Vai Mata (see figures 4.9–4.12). As opposed to the ahu that were constructed of rough stones that were laid randomly, the ones that were beautifully crafted used level cubes, well-wrought stone with joints so thin and fitted with such precision that they can hardly be penetrated by a knife, representing an art form of the highest order.

The best example of this extraordinary masonry art is found at Ahu Tahiri in Vinapu (see figure 4.12), located on the southeast coast at the foot of Rano Kau.[3] Here the masonry joints are so precise as to be almost imperceptible, and the face of the stones have a slightly convex surface. The stones are generally rectangular,

but some are carved in other shapes and fitted together like a perfect jigsaw puzzle. Some blocks were so huge that they could not have been shifted by the mason to find out whether they fit or not. Therefore, they must have been tooled to precise size before being set. This work must have been accomplished by the grinding of the stones with sand and water, plus an abundance of skill and patience.

Visitors to Vinapu have been struck by the similarity observed between the masonry of the seaside wall of Ahu Tahiri and the megalithic monuments found in the central Andes of South America—the finely cut stone found in the walls of pre-Inca Cuzco and in the Tiahuanaco masonry and statuary. For decades, because of this, a possible relationship between Easter Island and South American architecture has been suggested.

Thor Heyerdahl, the famous Norwegian explorer, makes a strong case in his many writings for an American origin to many of the cultural elements found on Easter Island.[4] The kneeling statue found at Rano Raraku quarries has been compared to the kneeling statues of Tiahuanaco. These are seen as mental templates or early prototypes brought from South America that climaxed in the standardized and highly stylized statues of Easter Island's Rano Raraku.

Heyerdahl also postulated that Easter Island experienced several periods of building, the earliest of which exhibited the fine stonework at structures like the one at Vinapu, which were the result of an early American influence, not existing in any other Polynesian island.[5] For many observers these similarities seem more than a coincidence and are a clear indication that there was some form of inspiration from South America. However, the analysis of radiocarbon dated ahu structures support their Polynesian origin and that they represent—in the words of William Mulloy—an "unbroken chronological progression such as might be expected from the architectural reflection of the activities of a single continuously developing society."[6] Mulloy's model, which also involved the idea of complex cultural evolution processes under extreme or total isolation, was adopted by several authors in the mid-1990s.

Roger C. Green stated that a model of essential cultural continuity for the prehistoric Easter Island sequence from the time of its colonization is "one common to and supported by the evidence from all

Figure 4.10. Detail of precisely fitted blocks at Ahu Tepeu.

Figure 4.11. The base of Ahu Tepeu's seaside wall has giant stones beautifully fitted together.

Figure 4.12. An extremely tight fit between adjacent stones at Ahu Tahiri in Vinapu, an incredibly skilled work of stone masonry. As with Ahu Tepeu, the stonework resembles the fine masonry also found in Peru's Inca empire.

Figure 4.13. Tahai ceremonial complex.

the islands of East Polynesia."[7] However, he discards the idea that Easter Island remained culturally isolated and, as we believe, suggests that Easter Island experienced multiple and continued contacts with other east Polynesian islands, in particular from the Mangareva, Henderson, and Pitcairn region.[8]

After a broad examination of the topic of Rapanui origins, Green indicates that the hypothesis of "an East Polynesian origin with later possible contacts with South America proves to be far more strongly supported than the others."[9] It has been established that two plants of South American origin—the sweet potato arriving by AD 1000 and the bottle gourd probably arriving around the AD twelfth century—appeared in Eastern Polynesia prior to their European distribution. In regards to the plant evidence, Green cites Yen's argument that "only the sweet potato among the prehistoric crop plants was capable of supporting the kind of society that is visualized as producing the structural esoterica of Easter Island."[10] Then he goes on and says that "these constructions were not present in the period AD 800–1110, but present thereafter, together with a sizeable population. Thus, while the Easter Island sequence does not require the presence of the sweet potato in its crops at the time of established settlement, it does seem to require it to be present some centuries after that event, and well before AD 1200."[11]

Regardless of their ultimate origin, if the distinct monumental architecture of the ahu developed in Easter Island around AD 1100–1200, there would be no chronological discrepancy. It's clear that the complexity and size of image ahu workmanship increased greatly through time. Façades reached thirty feet high as in the ahu at the Tahai ceremonial complex.[12] Taken as a whole these monumental structures represent an architectural achievement suggestive of a culture with a considerable coercive political organization.

Ahu Tongariki was the largest ceremonial structure ever built on Easter Island. In terms of size, plan, and the number of statues, it represents the apogee in the development of the image ahu, most of which were built in a period of approximately five hundred years between circa AD 1200–1700.

This monument is one of the most spectacular expressions of prehistoric megalithic ceremonial architecture in the entire Polynesian culture. With a central platform close to three hundred feet long and two lateral extensions or wings with frontal access ramps, this ahu originally had a total length of approximately 720 feet. The average height of the massive seaward wall was over 13 feet and used more than eight hundred crude and irregularly fitted basalt blocks. During its final phase of construction and function as a ceremonial altar, the central platform of Ahu Tongariki supported fifteen monolithic statues of volcanic tuff, carved at and transported from the moai quarries of Rano Raraku volcano, about 0.62 miles to the northwest (see figures 4.13–4.16). The Ahu Tongariki statues have heights ranging from more than 16 to almost 29 feet. Their average weight was over forty-four tons, with the largest statue, placed near the central section of the platform, weighing an estimated ninety-seven tons. With the statues raised on top of the platform and crowned by large topknots of red scoria (*pukao*), the monument had the impressive height of close to 46 feet.[13]

The image ahu, with their giant moai, were symbols of power, prestige, and the status of a lineage or tribe. Therefore, one way to display the destruction of another group during a war would be to destroy their ahu and its statues. Archaeological data, oral traditions, ethnography, historical documents, and architectural analysis all suggest that ahu were intentionally destroyed or deeply modified as a consequence of intertribal warfare during the late prehistoric times.

During late prehistoric and early historic times the great majority of image ahu became burial places. Stone vaults or cists with secondary burials were built inside some ahu platforms or excavated into the ramps and ahu plazas. Access to these funereal areas was restricted, as it was tapu (taboo) for the great majority of the population. Routledge indicates that the study of the ahu is simplified by the fact that they were still being used in living memory for the purpose for which they were doubtless originally built. They have been termed "burial places," but burial in its usual sense was not their only nor, in most cases, their principal purpose. A corpse was wrapped in a tapa blanket and then enclosed and wrapped in a mattress of reeds; fishhooks, chisels, and other objects were sometimes included. Bound into a bundle, it was then carried on staves to the ahu, where it was exposed in an oblong framework. The framework consisted of four corner uprights set in

Figure 4.14. Ahu Tongariki after total restoration, with the ahu as seen from the coast.

Figure 4.15. A view from the plaza of moai figures of Ahu Tongariki after total restoration.

the ground; its upper extremities were Y-shaped and two transverse bars rested in the bifurcated ends— one at the head, the other at the foot—and on these transverse bars were placed the ends of the bundle that wrapped the corpse.[14]

After the destruction of most image ahu and the deliberate overthrowing of their statues (see figure 4.16), these sites continued to be used for burials, deeply altering the original structure, until they were left in ruins upon conversion of the population to Catholicism in the second half of the nineteenth century.

Semi-Pyramid Ahu

Many of the ruined image ahu were converted into enormous heaps of stones (*tumuli*) almost completely covering the previous structure. These and other structures originally built resembling a low pyramid cut in two are known as semi-pyramid ahu. Here the section that is the rear wall forms a triangle with its inland-inclined slopes. Their height is 5 to 12 feet and the largest structures of this type vary in length from 100 to 160 feet. Though these are commonly called ahu, they were basically collective funerary structures. Beneath these large masses of stones and the large overthrown statues, funerary vaults or cists were built. Routledge reports thirteen semi-pyramid ahu made from older image ahu and, in addition, approximately fifty to sixty semi-pyramid style ahu on the island.[15] There is no precise knowledge as to when this type of structure was developed, nor to indicate whether or not some of these were contemporary with the image ahu; however, many show evidence of having been in use into the first half of the nineteenth century.

Ahu Poepoe

The name of this type of ahu derives from its elongated form and curved raised ends which resemble the bow and stern of a ship, suggesting these stone structures were probably constructed after discovery of the island by Europeans in the eighteenth century. Métraux indicates that oral traditions make reference to a man, expert in the construction of this type of ahu, among the people kidnapped by the Peruvian slave raids in 1862.[16] Like the semi-pyramid ahu, ahu poepoe also contain collective funerary remains. Constructed of carefully selected stones, some closely fitting but not cut, they have narrow funerary vaults in the interior extending along the length of the structure. They total about a dozen and are found on the north coast.

Ahu poepoe are wedge shaped and usually have their long axis oriented perpendicularly, with its highest point aiming toward the coast (see figure 4.21). Some have a white stone, a broken piece of a statue of Rano Raraku tuff, or a lump of red scoria set up as a marker in the center of the ramp. These were reported by Routledge informants to be signs that the area was tapu out of respect for the dead.[17]

Rectangular Ahu

This type of ahu is a rectangular heap of irregular stones, with a flat surface and funerary vaults in the interior (see figure 4.22). Sebastian Englert reports twenty of these structures and indicates they are also known as *avanga*, a term that denotes any type of burial in general.[18] Métraux refers to these structures as "a type that, though not common, exists in several places along the north coast. These structures differ from the wedge-shaped variety ahu poepoe in that their upper surfaces are flat rather than sloping. Ahu Avanga Vai-porotu, situated on a sea cliff near Vai-tara-kai-ua, is a typical rectangular ahu."[19]

RESIDENTIAL DWELLINGS

In the daytime, Easter Island is bright, and the immense vault of the sky melts at the horizon into the endless sea creating an almost buoyant sensation in the beholder. The natives spent the day under this bright, expansive heaven. But when darkness fell, they crawled through a low tunnel to sleep in a highly confined, windowless, pitch-black space. The ancient Rapanui architects may have subconsciously created this dark, confined sleeping space to provide a welcome contrast to the bright, sunlit expanse that was their stage for daytime living.

Prehistoric Easter Island had four primary types of dwellings: caves, pole houses, thatched shelters (such as the boathouse), and stone houses.

Cave (ana) Dwellings

Easter Island contains numerous caves in a variety of forms and sizes, plus grottoes and crannies. Those along the coast were often used as permanent family

Figure 4.16. A section of Ahu Tongariki's rear wall exhibiting nine of its fifteen statues. Authors Patricia Vargas Casanova and Claudio Cristino can be seen in the foreground working at the site.

Figure 4.17. Northeast side of Ahu Tongariki, with all statues aligned on the central platform.

Figure 4.18. A destroyed image ahu at Hanga Te'e, also called Ahu Vaihu. The best-preserved figures lie on their faces in their exact position after their fall.

Figure 4.19. Image ahu at Hanga Te'e. After the deliberate overthrowing of the stone sculptures, their red topknots, which were delicately balanced on their heads, rolled onto the plaza.

Figure 4.20. A semi-pyramid ahu on the north coast.

dwellings, overnight shelters during fishing expeditions, treasure depositors, or burial places. Inside the caves, archaeologists have found all types of implements for everyday living and fishing including spearheads, needles, and seashells. The caves often had architectural embellishments more comfortable than one might think. Their entrances were often protected by stone walls to make them more difficult to find or for intruders to enter. Within there were sometimes terraced floors, sleeping platforms covered with straw for comfort, and stone pillows (*ngarua*). The interiors often had walls and ceilings covered in white plaster. The art within the caves varied from painted pictures, petroglyphs, or stone bas-reliefs to engraved drawings.

Some caves are not deep or well enclosed, but are merely overhanging shelters. Around these caves, low vertical stone walls were added above ground with stone roofs in places that otherwise would be exposed to the sky. Many are circular in shape with natural rock, flat corbelled stone, and earthen roofs, such as those built in the Tahai ceremonial area. Some were divided into living units to be occupied by one or several families. They were entered from the side, typically through a long, low, narrow tunnel. The interior walls and floor consisted of either the cave's natural rough surface or finely finished and fitted stonework. At one

time, according to the explorer Don Felipe González in 1770, "most of the natives of the island dwell[ed] in underground caves."[20]

Many more caves are found inland, formed by the flow and cooling of lava during the island's volcanic past. Some caves called *ana kionga* were modified to provide a retreat during periods of war. Again, the entranceway was a stone architectural addition, narrow and downward sloping, making it difficult to gain access to the cave (see figure 4.26). This entranceway could easily be closed by erecting simple stone walls to form a perfect place for defeated clans to hide after a battle. Cut dressed stones were added to these natural rock caves to divide the interior space into complete rooms, some of oval shape, similar to the common thatched boathouse.

The entrances of many other caves exhibit complex architectural additions and were deeply modified with the construction of a thick stone wall, leaving only a narrow passage allowing access to their interior chambers (see figure 4.27).

Some caves and their entrances were family secrets. Each family had one or more caves whose whereabouts were known to only one family member. To divulge such information was thought to bring severe punishment from the gods to the transgressor.

Figure 4.21. A wedge-shaped type of ahu poepoe on the north coast.

Within the cave's little nooks and crannies, the islanders stored provisions, utensils, and sacred objects such as rongo-rongo tablets and small stone and wooden statues. The reasons for secreting such effects would have been various, but the most likely were to preserve them for their rituals or simply to preserve family treasures.

Other caves often served as burial chambers. Corpses buried in the caves were wrapped in tapa and guarded the family treasure. Some corpses had chisels and fish-hooks wrapped within their tapa.

Pole Houses

The earliest dwelling besides a cave was the wooden pole house. The European discoverers saw the natives dwelling in such houses, portrayed here as conjectural illustrations in figures 4.29a, b, c, d, following Roggeveen's description:

Their houses or huts are without any ornamentation, and have a length of fifty feet and a width of fifteen; the height being nine feet, as it appears by guess. The construction of their walls, as we saw in the framework of a new building, is begun with stakes which are stuck into the ground and secured straight upright, across with other long strips of wood which I may call laths are lashed, to the height of four or five, thus completing the framework of the building. Then the interstices, which are all of oblong shape, are closed up and covered over with a sort of rush or long grass, which they put on very thickly, layer upon layer, and fasten on the inner side with lashings (which they know how to make from a certain field product called Piet, very neatly and skillfully, and is in no way inferior to our own thin cord); so that they are always as well shut against wind and rain as those who live beneath thatched roofs in Holland. These dwellings have no more than one entrance way, which is so low that they pass in creeping on their knees, being round above, as a vault or archway; the roof is also of the same form . . . these long huts admit no daylight except through the one entrance-way, and are destitute of windows and closely shut in all around . . . It only remains to say, in concluding the subject of these dwelling-huts, that we did not see more than six or seven of them at the place where we landed, from which it may clearly be inferred that all the Indians make use of their possessions in common, for the large size and small number of their dwellings give one to know that many live together and slept in a single building.[21]

Figure 4.22. At Vai Mata, a rectangular funerary structure built on the plaza of an image ahu transformed into a semi-pyramidal ahu.

Figure 4.23. The semi-pyramid ahu resemble a pyramid cut in two, so that the seawall forms a triangle.

Figure 4.24. A natural overhang shelter with a large terrace defined by a low retaining wall at the Tahai ceremonial area.

Figure 4.25. Cave dwellings were often built with flat stone roofs, in this case covered with turf. Stone walls defined their shape and structurally upheld the roof.

The site of one wooden pole house was excavated in 1987 by Patricia Vargas Casanova with an archaeological team from the University of Chile in the environs of Anakena Beach.[22] They found the remains of ancient postholes forming a perfect circular plan, twenty feet in diameter, suggesting the existence of a pole house in the late seventeenth century (see figures 4.29a, b, c, d).

This pole house probably had a steeply sloped, thatched roof resting on a cluster of poles at the center. This type of shelter must have prevailed during the early settlement period of Easter Island. It was later abandoned as a construction method when mature trees became increasingly scarce and the boathouse became the predominant residential form on the coastal plains.

In 1786, the French explorers La Pérouse and Bernizet described two contemporary types of dwellings, both with an ellipsoid form. One type near the coast was built of rough stones without mortar; the other type was the pole house. The pole houses were situated in the middle of extensive plantations, built in the form of an elongated ellipse and very narrow in proportion to their length. La Pérouse, as quoted in Heyerdahl, refers to a large reed house situated near the landing place in Hanga Roa Bay: "This house is large enough to contain upwards of two hundred persons. It is not the dwelling of a chief, for it is without furniture, and so great a space would be useless to him. It forms a village by itself, with the addition of two or three other small houses at a little distance"[23] (see figures 4.29a, b, c, d).

Bernizet, the expedition engineer, measured and described that house in detail:

The foundations . . . consist of square stones sunk in the earth, about two feet long and six inches thick, having holes at certain distances destined

Figure 4.26. Many cave's entrances were modified with the construction of a thick stone wall, leaving only a narrow access passage.

Figure 4.27. Some caves exhibit complex architectural additions, with a vertical entranceway to a narrow tunnel descending underground into the cave.

to receive the poles, that serve to cross beams . . . which terminate the roof, and are still further strengthened by the uprights . . . driven into the ground at the distance of ten feet from each other. The poles are bound together, through their whole length, by transversal laths, placed at a distance of two feet. The highest point is in the centre; and a plane, supposed to pass through the summit, perpendicular to the large axis of the ellipse, would have the form of a semi-ellipse. The whole is covered with rushes, from nine to ten inches in diameter at the lower end, and bound together, so as to form mats, by means of cords twisted with the hand. The two doors, of which there is one on each side, are not larger than those of the small huts, and the oven . . . on the windward side, is guarded by a palisading. . . . The form of these large buildings, however, cannot be considered invariable; for some of them, either in the plan or elevation are more bent than the curve of the ellipse.[24]

Boathouses and Other Thatched Houses

The Easter Islanders had to design an architectural form that would conserve the remaining smaller trees by only using small branches and twigs. This type was called a boathouse by the Europeans, named for its resemblance to an overturned canoe with an upward pointed keel. Thus, it seems that, in a relatively short period, house architecture evolved from the large pole house type with vertical walls to the narrow

boathouse designs with curved walls described by Jacob Roggeveen in 1722 (see figure 4.29a) and Don Juan Hervé in 1770 (see figure 4.29c). Apparently these houses became smaller over time, and as illustrated by Pierre Loti in 1872 (see figure 4.35), one hundred years later, they were reduced to almost one-third their size (see figures 4.29a, b, c, d and 4.34a, b).[25]

Loti's illustration seems to be taken from real life with little artistic additions, suggesting a desire to reveal a lot (see figure 4.35). The chief standing on the left is a strong, well-built man with well-developed legs, suggesting exercise and work. He is clothed with a simple loincloth and a long robe touching the ground and tied in front with a carved ornament. He is bearded with a feathered headdress bending in the wind while resting on a long ceremonial stave with a carved wooden head on top. The stave, headdress, and cloak are symbols of his authority. A beautiful woman is cooking under a rounded, wind-breaking thatched shelter, supported by a stick resting in a forked brace. The boathouse is small and low with a single small entrance flanked by two stone sculptures that are the ceremonial guards. The man on the right with a hairpiece is touching one of the sculptures as either a symbol of respect or as a religious practice, assuming the statues represent an ancestral god. The barefooted person entering the house is crawling headfirst and is in Western dress, indicating he is one of the explorers. The villagers in the background are curiously observing the visitor, as is the chief. The curved rafters of the boathouse were either stuck directly into the ground, or in the homes of wealthier or aristocratic families, into holes carved in rows of low curbstone.

Figure 4.28. The cave shown in figure 4.27, photographed here from the interior, showing its miniscule, narrow entrance. Small and protective entrances were common in all island residential designs.

This type of boathouse, called hare paenga, comprised the principal dwelling type of Easter Island's elite class of chiefs and nobility during its Golden Age. The curbstones, varying in number from fifteen to seventy and a sign of wealth, were worked to define the outer oval circumference of the dwelling, creating a beautiful elliptical shape. From these highly prized curbstones sprang the curved wooden framework. In times of war the triumphant party probably carried off the curbstones of the defeated party's abandoned village.

The boathouse's perfectly elliptical floor plan and semicircular front stoop was an example of the use of pure geometry by the architects of Easter Island. The boathouse was an oval structure where walls and roof were one. It was built without windows or other openings except for the singular entranceway, making the interior dark and cool.

The boathouse was an inflated ellipse, resting, in most cases, directly on the ground, supported by a light wooden framework containing a ridgepole, rafters, and purlins. This roof and wall assembly was covered by thatch, made up of successive layers of reed, grass, and sugar cane. The floors were dirt or grass, materials more comfortable than stone for sleeping.

As twigs abounded in all lengths, it was logical that the Easter Islanders would exploit this fact in arriving at the design of their principal residential unit in the coastal plains. The inverted boat-shape design was the result. At either end of the boathouse, they put the shortest branches, graduating to longer ones as they built toward the center.

The boathouse doorway was a unique tunnel entrance located in the middle of the house, usually on the seaward side, projecting forward a few feet perpendicular to the house. The long opening was approximately eighteen to twenty-four inches high and required anyone entering to crawl on all fours or on one's belly. Intruders were rendered defenseless in such a position—easy to repel with a stone or club. The entrance tunnel also provided protection from the rain but let in a cool breeze. Since the dwelling's primary purpose was for sleeping, the interior was dark. The ceiling was too low to permit walking. On either side of the entranceway, there were two parallel curbs at the center of the semicircular porch. Occasionally, two small stone pillars or stone statues graced either side of the entrance.

The thatch superstructure of the boathouse was light and sturdy, and since the islanders were faced with a shortage of wood, it could easily be moved when the clan abandoned one village site for another.

The various wooden elements of the frame were lashed together by ropes of hau bark (*hahau*), always with an odd number of knots because even numbers were considered bad luck. The thatch roofing was securely fastened to the wood to resist the island's strong winds and rain. Sometimes the inner layer of roofing consisted of mats (similar to the sleeping mats, made of rushes sewn together with cords) then covered with sugarcane leaves and finally with grass.

According to Routledge's informants, the people slept parallel to the axis of the house with their heads facing the door. The older people slept in the center and the younger ones toward each end. In general the interior spaces had few furnishings since they were used solely for sleeping. General family activities were performed outside in the fresh air. They must have enjoyed the freedom of the open space in the family compound or in the larger communal village.

Apparently the Easter Islanders used these houses solely for sleeping and storing possessions. When an important house was built, it was inaugurated by the village chief and a priest, the custodians of tradition. They were the first to eat in the dwelling, but only if it was a prominent house—a house with a stone foundation.

Later, however, the hare paenga lost their special status, as they remained in use as regular houses by the surviving population up to the nineteenth century. The islanders' design of the boathouse combined the exquisite and sensuous elliptical floor plan with the

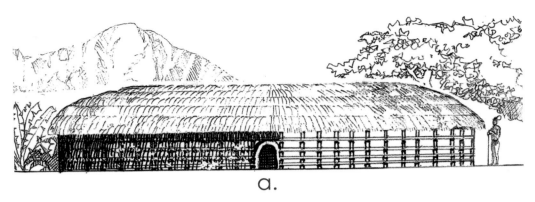

a.

Figure 4.29*a.* Hypothetical reconstruction by Kenneth Treister of the pole-house residential type described in 1722 by Roggeveen for Easter Island (after Vargas Casanova et al. 1992).

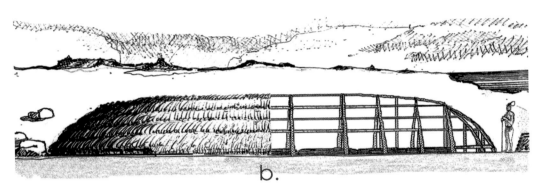

b.

Figure 4.29*b.* Hypothetical reconstruction by Kenneth Treister of a large elliptical house with paenga (stone foundations) also known as hare aio, located on the north coast of the island (after Vargas Casanova et al. 1992).

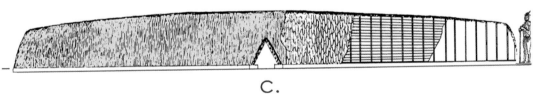

c.

Figure 4.29*c.* A large elliptical house (hare paenga) drawn by Hervé in 1770, on the southeast coast. Illustration created by Kenneth Treister.

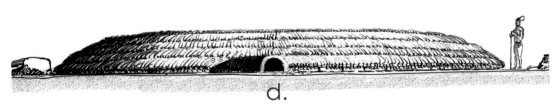

d.

Figure 4.29*d.* Hypothetical reconstruction by Kenneth Treister of a hare paenga on the southeast coast based on the 1981 archaeological survey records by Claudio Cristino and Patricia Vargas Casanova.

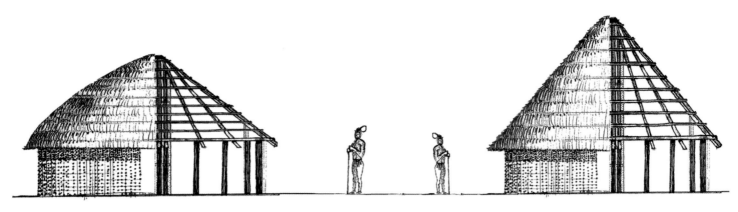

Figure 4.30*a, b.* Conjectural reconstructions of a prehistoric thatched pole house, circular in plan, based on ancient post holes found at Anakena by archaeologist Patricia Vargas Casanova. Illustration created by Kenneth Treister.

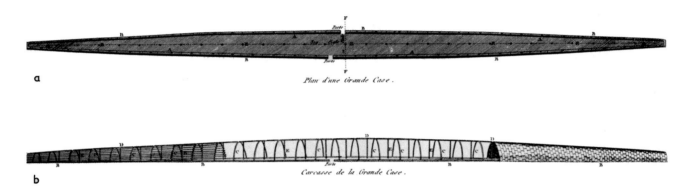

Figure 4.31. Easter Island dwelling structure in 1786. This large reed house (about 320 feet long) was situated near the landing place in Hanga Roa. Photo from the 1786 La Pérouse expedition as published in Heyerdahl and and Ferdou, eds., *Archaeology of Easter Island*, 1:60.

semicircular patio to create complementary architectural shapes that exhibit a high degree of indigenous aesthetic expression.

Outside each boathouse was a half-moon shaped patio. These patios were up to nine feet wide and paved with large, matched, rounded water-worn boulders, hand-selected from the sea, similar to those found on the top surface of the ahu. The patio was level and well drained and during the rainy season helped keep people's feet dry and mud from being brought into the house. This patio provided a neat architectonic platform on which the natives could sit, talk, and perform their daily activities with cooking nearby. Rock decorations and stone benches often enhanced this communal area.

Symmetry and geometry were surprising tools in the island's architectural vocabulary. Some of the residential houses were of a rectangular plan. The external pavement was also rectangular, composed of flat, irregular

stones situated outside the house (see figure 4.46 top). The remains of about 400 rectangular houses and 150 houses of circular plan were found among the ravines of Maunga Tere Vaka, across the high grounds of the Island's interior.

Larger boathouses (*hare nui*)—also called "feast houses"—were built for a special festivity (*koro*) given for a father either living or dead. The feast was the material symbol of generosity and camaraderie. "In connection with the koro is always mentioned a big house, also called hare koro, where young people spent their time playing various games. This house was the material symbol of the generosity of the koro giver. Tradition has preserved descriptions of koro houses, which were several hundred feet long and more than twenty feet high."[26]

Written accounts by European explorers during the eighteenth century confirmed these observations and described feast houses as having two small doorways

Figures 4.32*a, b, c.* Various views of boathouse curbstone foundations.

Figure 4.33. Boathouse foundations and patio in the Tahai ceremonial complex.

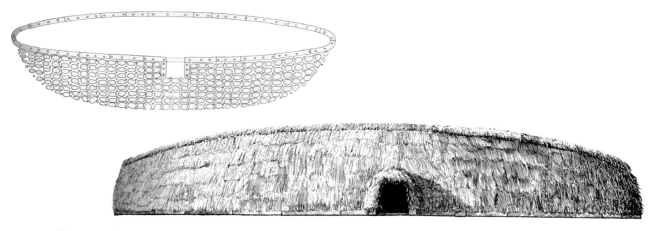

Figures 4.34a, b. Boathouse: Plan view above and conjectural elevation below. After Mulloy, in Heyerdahl and Ferdou, eds., *Archaeology of Easter Island*, 1:145.

on either side of the structure but not exactly opposite. Food was served in abundance and passed hand-to-hand through the entrances at each end or through small side openings and eaten in the house in the darkness. Sometimes there were more than ten earth ovens cooking sweet potatoes and chickens at the same time. The festival lasted many days, even months. Routledge tells us that during the koro festivals, "The old people sang, the young people danced, and the host who lived in a little house nearby came and looked on. On the last day there was a great feast, and when it was done, the koro house was torn down with the aid of symbolic, carved wooden lizards."[27]

In the late nineteenth century, soon after the first Western explorers settled on the island, the use of the boathouse completely disappeared and the natives either lived in huts made of wood from wrecked ships, copies of European cabins, or caves, with furnishings similar to those of the boathouse.

FURNISHINGS

Furnishings within the residential structures included straw mats or grass floors, stone pillows, gourds for holding water, baskets for food, and wooden images and tablets hanging from the ceiling. The mats (*moenga*) were made of reed and fine specimens were highly valued. The square stone pillows were often decorated with straight lines or with a stylized representation of the vulva. Stone pillows were not used elsewhere in Polynesia. The Easter Islanders had no ceramics, although they did carve bowls and other containers from stone.[28]

DOMESTIC FAMILY COMPOUND

The late prehistoric domestic family compound was usually composed of a main house (*hare*) of elliptical plan, several hearths for cooking (*umu pae*), agricultural structures (*manavai*) for protecting the crops, and stone chicken houses (*hare moa*) to protect the domesticated chickens.

OVENS

One small but interesting architectural element found in all the villages and the agricultural areas was the stone oven. The oven is usually pentagonal or heptagonal in shape, with five or seven stone slabs forming a curb. The odd number has superstitious significance as mentioned before, so only a few ovens were made of six stones. The curbs were buried in the ground about five inches and enclosed a space approximately two feet in diameter.

These ovens were used to cook meats, sweet potatoes, yams, and taro (a tropical Asian plant of the arum family that has edible starchy corms and edible fleshy leaves, especially a variety with a large central corm used as a staple in the Pacific). Their bottom was constructed of large stones over which grass, branches, and scraps of wood were placed with smaller stones on top. This was ignited and the heated stones were subsequently spread around and over the food wrapped and protected by banana leaves. Soil was then shoveled over the pit, and several hours later the cooked food was removed.

Archaeological remains around the ovens contain few fish bones, indicating that fish was a delicacy and

Figure 4.35. An elliptical house (hare paenga) drawn by Pierre Loti in 1872. After Loti, in Heyerdahl and Ferdou, eds., *Archaeology of Easter Island*, 1:77.

not a staple in the islander's diet. Fishing must have been difficult because of the shortage of wood for building boats, the rough coastal cliffs, the lack of natural lagoons or harbors, the lack of an offshore protective coral reef, and the fact that fishing near the island was generally poor. During the period when the British company Williamson and Balfour leased the island from Chile, the natives had to get written permission to fish off their own island!

The main ingredient in the Easter Islanders' diet after approximately AD 1100 was the sweet potato. This tuber thrived in Easter Island's well-drained, porous soil. As one Easter Islander stated in the last century, "Here we begin at birth by eating sweet potatoes and then we keep eating sweet potatoes, and then finally we die."[29]

CHICKEN HOUSES

The Easter Islanders prized the chicken and used it for currency and gifts. To protect their fowl, they built large rectangular stone coops. These so-called chicken houses or hare moa had an interior with a long, narrow chamber reached by one or more tiny openings. At night the entrance was closed with stones. Anyone attempting to steal a chicken would have to remove the stones, making a noise that would alert the nearby owner sleeping in his dwelling.

Chicken houses were part of domestic compounds and usually are found in close association with agricultural structures. They are rectangular stone structures with inclined double walls and rounded ends filled with gravel. The structure sat on a heavy stone foundation.

A total of 1,233 chicken houses were found and documented all over the island.[30] These structures dominate much of the landscape in the coastal plains and, as Diamond said, "If it were not for the fact that Easter's abundant big stone hare moa are overshadowed by its even bigger stone platforms and statues, tourists would remember Easter as the island of stone chicken houses . . . because today the prehistoric stone chicken houses—all 1,233 of them—are much more conspicuous than the prehistoric human houses, which had only stone foundations or patios and no stone walls."[31]

CATCH BASINS

There were few water sources except rain on the island, which accumulated in crater lakes, and the nature of its volcanic geology is such that water runs through the surface quickly like a porous sieve. Therefore, shallow stone catch basins called *taheta* were used to collect and hold precious rainwater. Some were simply scooped out of the stone and others elaborately carved into oval, rectangular, and circular shapes (see figures 4.40 and 4.41).

Figure 4.36. Paved, semicircular patio of a boathouse (hare paenga) in Tahai, paved with large, rounded boulders (maea poro).

Figure 4.37. A pentagonal umu pae, a characteristic feature of households from the coastal plains.

AGRICULTURAL ENCLOSURES

The island is peppered with semicircular, circular, and rectangular stone enclosures (*manavai*) that were used as cultivation enclosures to protect valuable plants for the ancient Rapanui society. The paper mulberry trees used for making tapa (the inner bark of the tree, which, when pounded, produces a paper-like cloth) for loincloths and also banana trees were grown within these walled enclosures. The stone walls protected the frail trees from the harsh southern winds, kept salinity away, and conserved the much-needed moisture. They are usually associated with domestic compounds. Some were on the surface, some partially underground, while others were completely below the ground level, the tops of the plants at surface level. Some were built independently while others were in groups up to forty in number. All types seem to represent an adaptive response to the island's ecology.[32]

Figure 4.38. Although they were built with their long axis parallel to the direction of the slope, both chicken houses (hare moa) are leveled on top.

Figure 4.39. Two hare moa were found on the north coast. In the center of the structure above, a small rectangular entrance gives access to a narrow interior chamber.

A partial or fully underground manavai was built where natural depressions were located. They had simple walls built with superimposed rocks surrounded by a dirt mound formed after deepening the natural features of the land surface.

Where stony ground made it difficult or impossible to create the dirt mound, large agricultural areas and taro gardens within the lithic mulch were defined by circular depressions and cut directly into the land surface.

Houses with circular plans were probably temporary structures for seasonal use. Some of these had foundations of basalt slabs with a concentric circle of horizontal external paving. In both types, the enclosures above ground were built with a light wooden framework supporting thatched walls that were also the roofs.

Along the shore near the ancient settlements were stone towers, whose true use is a mystery although they were identified by some as turtle watchtowers and also are thought to be the dwellings of specialized priests who carried out observations of the stars. It has been said that astronomical observations were used to determine the beginning of the lunar year, the time of planting, harvesting, and religious festivities, and also to predict changes in the equatorial marine current associated with the arrival of the turtles, migratory birds, and fish.

Some of these watchtowers stood ten feet high and measured up to twenty-three feet in diameter. They were laid with loose, rough stones and spanned inside by crude corbel vaults, with sleeping apartments in the lower chambers. As in other types of dwellings, the entrance was a low, narrow passage (see figure 4.48).

Figure 4.40. A simple catch basin carved from the natural stone.

Figure 4.41. Catch basins were carved in different types of rock and in varying sizes and shapes.

Figure 4.42. A partially underground agricultural enclosure showing a simple wall surrounded by a dirt mound formed after excavation to deepen the natural depression. This enclosure is protecting a banana tree whose floppy leaves are susceptible to wind damage.

Figure 4.43. Surface agricultural enclosure (manavai) walls on the southeast coastal plains.

Figure 4.44. Detail of an agricultural enclosure's stone construction.

Figure 4.45. A surface manavai built using the characteristic vaka ure construction system: a thick double wall with gravel fill (kikiri) in the interior.

Figure 4.46. In the high grounds of the island the foundations of hundreds of houses with rectangular and circular plans are still visible. The picture at the center (right) shows a hypothetical reconstruction of the thatched roof and walls of a rectangular house. Photos by Patricia Vargas Casanova and illustrations by Patricia Vargas Casanova, Claudio Cristino, and Roberto Izaurieta.

In 1774, Forster, one of Captain Cook's naturalists, stated, "we observed some heaps of stones piled up into little hillocks, which had one steep perpendicular side, where a hole went underground. The space within could be very small, and yet it is probable that these cavities likewise served to give shelter to the people during the night . . . We should have been glad to have ascertained this circumstance, but the natives always denied us admittance into these places."[33] In 1786, Anthony Bernizet describes a tower that had a wing containing an inner chamber twenty-four feet long by six feet wide and seven feet high in the center. The walls were four feet thick and the door measured two feet by two feet.[34]

These towers might have been used as lookouts for the movement of turtles or to locate schools of fish for fisherman at sea. Images of turtles were carved on the rocks nearby, which reinforced the legend about turtle watching. But their actual use is still a mystery. For one, as Alfred Métraux argues, the towers do not offer any better view of the sea or coastline than do the nearby hills. Also, turtles were not common on Easter Island. Why then were they built? The towers thus form a strange architectural question among the many mysteries clouding Easter Island. No architectural counterpart in the rest of Polynesia exists except for some similarity to the fishermen's shrines in Hawaii.

THE SACRED STONE VILLAGE OF ORONGO

During the late prehistoric period Orongo was the ceremonial center of the Birdman Cult. Here the Easter Island natives built an entire village of beautiful stone houses grouped into long, low one-story apartment-type buildings. These buildings were used only once a year during the cult's festivities.

The picturesque site of Orongo has fifty-three dwellings parading along the top of a thin ridge. A series of pedestrian walks, defined by the long continuous blocks of dwelling units, interconnects the buildings and creates the feeling of a unified village (see figure 4.51). The vertical walls of the one-story façades of each building use geometric shapes—circles, rectangles, semicircles, and staggered straight lines—to form an orderly, simple, and aesthetically pleasing linear design (see figures 4.51–4.53).

The stone dwellings at Orongo, some cut into the hillside, were made for sleeping only and are generally elliptical in shape. They are constructed of thick stone walls composed of horizontal thin slabs of rock set without mortar, covered with a layer of earth and grass. This not only insulated the structures but made the architecture part of the natural setting when approached from the hillside.

The village lies on the eastern slope of, and 650 feet above, the volcanic crater lake of Rano Kau. The half-mile-wide lake has the beautifully varied colors of totora reeds and green algae. Orongo also looks to the sea where the deep blue of the Pacific merges with the equally blue subtropical sky. The entire magnificent scene focuses on three small offshore islets (see figures 2.6 and 2.7) where the nesting seabirds—the sooty terns and great frigate birds—flock each year.

Overlooking and guarding the sea and the three offshore islands there is a special group of houses occupied by the priests watching the Birdman activities taking place on the offshore islands. These stone houses (see figures 4.55–4.57a, b) have a magical rhythm of a series of convex circular forms facing the sea. Another house (figures 4.58), probably for a special purpose, has a concave façade and is unique—lighter, almost classical in appearance, with its façade made up of a series of rhythmical openings formed by vertical column slabs. Also sharing the precipice are stone outcroppings that are carved with beautiful petroglyphs of the Birdman and other motifs (see figure 2.5). Petroglyphs found on rocks at the end of the village of Orongo represent the fantastic Birdman with the head of a frigate bird and a human body in a crouching position.

There are about three hundred loci with over a thousand petroglyphs found on the island—including sea animals, especially tuna—representing the island's graphic art.

Figure 4.47. A well-preserved tower at Hanga O Teo on the north coast. Note the typical single, low, narrow entrance.

Figure 4.48. Illustration of a stone and pit house from the 1797 La Pérouse expedition. Note the roof terrace is protected from wind and rain by having the northeast side wall higher than the rest. As published in Heyerdahl and Ferdou, eds., *Archaeology of Easter Island*, 1:59.

Figure 4.49. A well-built stone tower, silhouetted against the seas, seems to be a sentinel guarding the coast.

Figure 4.50. Location of a tupa on the north coast in the Hanga O Teo region.

Figure 4.51. Stone houses of the ceremonial village of Orongo. Their roofs are horizontal slabs covered with a thick layer of earth and grass. The architecture was integrated with the environment while articulating the use of architectural geometry (in this case the circle) on the roofs and seaside façades.

Figure 4.52. The stone houses at Orongo create a wonderful interlocking play of convex and concave shapes—pure sculpture.

Figure 4.53. The stone houses at Orongo with their entrances toward the sea and their turf roofs above. Turf roofs are used throughout the world in indigenous architecture to provide simple and quality insulation.

Figure 4.54. The interior of an Orongo stone house showing the corbeled roof in detail. On the far left side, note a pictorial representation of an ao, a dance paddle used by the chiefs and priests.

Figure 4.55. After restoration, one of the Orongo houses was left open to show its construction in detail.

Figure 4.56. This exposed structure shows how it supports a grass roof. Here architecture works with—and not opposed to—the natural landscape. The roofs are composed of thin, yet strong, slabs of stone held in place by seemingly precarious cantilevers of stone, a corbel, yet flat, vault. The equilibrium is so delicate that if one of the structural roof stones are broken or removed, the entire structure would probably collapse.

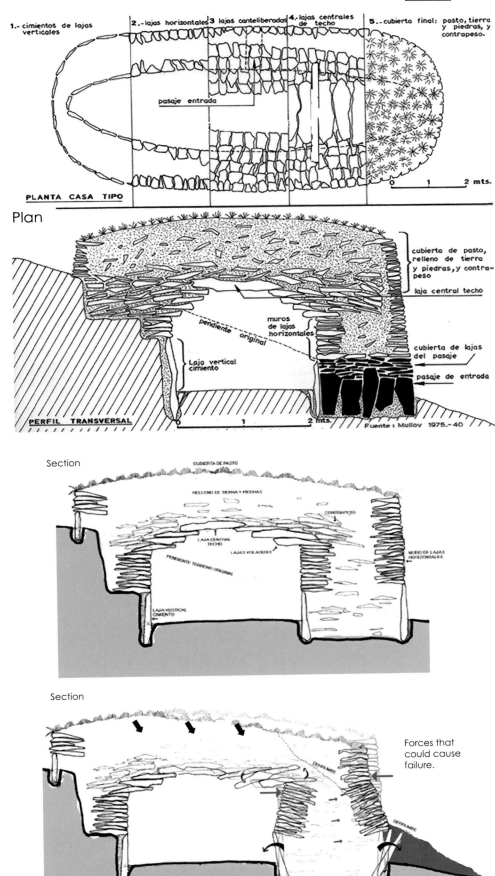

Plan

Section

Section

Forces that could cause failure.

Figures 4.57*a, b.* Schematic profiles showing an Orongo house's construction system and the forces that can cause basic structural failures.

Figure 4.58. A well-constructed, light, and relatively open house at Mata Ngarau in the southern corner of the village of Orongo.

Figure 4.59. Stone house at Mata Ngarau at Orongo. Detail of the series of openings supported by vertical stone-slab columns that create an unusual, open, and light façade.

Chapter 5

THE ART OF EASTER ISLAND

Figure 5.1. The east wall of the Rano Raraku volcano, where all the stone for the moai sculptures was quarried and carved.

IN the entire world there are few ancient structures as impressive as the moai statues and the quarries of Rano Raraku, the site where the stylized stone sculptures of Easter Island were created. These giant images of the native's founding chiefs created a dynamic relationship between the people and their ancestors. Facing the tribe's communal plaza, with their backs to the sea, they dominated the simple daily life of the natives.

These figures have long heads, the tops of which are flat, and the ears have lobes elongated almost to the chin. Elongation of the islanders' earlobes was common until the mid-1800s, and a couple of elders with extended earlobes were seen and photographed by Routledge in 1914. Elongation was achieved by inserting successively larger pegs in a hole pierced in the lobe, a practice also frequent among other Polynesian islanders. The fashion of piercing and distending the earlobe was prevalent also in the Maya civilization and with many other prehistoric people, particularly in Africa. Thor Heyerdahl says in his classic *The Art of Easter Island*, "A few islanders . . . claimed the ancestors of the present Atan family, claimed descent from the only adult male among the defeated and decimated group termed Long-Ears. This name was due to their custom of once artificially extending their earlobes as on the ahu images and the wooden moai kava-kava figures. The Long-Ears and the Short-Ears were said to have spoken

Figure 5.2. Giant statue at Rano Raraku quarry with its head carved and its sides and back still attached to its mother rock.

different languages and to have had different customs."[1] However, there is no genetic, linguistic, archaeological, or other cultural evidence supporting the idea of two different people settling on Rapa Nui.

Almost one thousand megalithic statues were carved on Easter Island, a number that sometimes exceeded the surviving population. Over the hundreds of years they were carved, their size increased from three feet in height to up to seventy-one feet tall, weighing over two hundred tons.

Since the early European contacts in the eighteenth century, these monumental statues captured visitors' attention and have been the subject of all kind of speculations, though systematic studies and inventories have a long history too.[2] In 1977, Cristino and Vargas Casanova, along with a University of Chile team, began the Easter Island Statuary Project as an integral part of the archaeological survey.[3] The Easter Island Statuary Project is the most comprehensive artifact inventory carried out to date on Easter Island. As fieldwork went on in 1978 and the number of recorded sculptures increased, fifty-five metric and stylistic attributes were identified as inclusively descriptive of a moai statue, and a data-recording technique, based upon the establishment of these discrete attributes, was developed. The technique was preliminarily applied and evaluated in 1979–1980 during the documentation of Rano Raraku quarries and has been in use since then. After five years of continuous fieldwork seasons, Vargas Casanova and Cristino had systematically described a total of 740 moai as archaeological features and identified them either as individual sites or features of complex sites. Following this field research, along with cartographer Izaurieta, in 1981 they published the *Atlas arqueológico de Isla de Pascua* (*Archaeological Atlas of Easter Island*), including a detailed map of Rano Raraku and the associated settlement within an area of 0.58 square miles around the volcano (original scale 1:2.500), with precise plan views of all statues located at the exterior quarries (section A), superior quarries (section B), and interior quarries (sections C and D), and clear identification of each of the quarries within those sections, including symbols at scale indicating location, orientation (head and base), and size of the 396 statues recorded in this area as well as the principal cuts, walls, and niches of each quarry.[4]

By 1987, this research team had accomplished the documentation and plotting in topographic maps of 818 moai statues and produced a thematic map of the Easter Island Statuary Project.[5] This thematic map indicated distribution and specific locations (ahu, quarry, in transport roads, and intermediate) as well as identified the materials (tuff, basalt, red scoria, and trachite) of all the recorded statues.

Subsequent stages of the statuary project were carried out in the following years. Between 1987 and 1988 another fifty-three statues were recorded in the west coast within sections of quadrants 26 and 32 in the north coast, at the Poike peninsula, and in the interior highlands at Maunga Tere Vaka included in quadrants 17 and 27 of the archaeological survey. Between 1989 and 1992, seventy-seven moai statues were documented in quadrant 21 and sections of quadrants 16, 20, 31, and 35 along the north coast. From 1993 onward, other statues were recorded in unsurveyed areas, and new statue fragments were discovered after the excavations and restoration works at Ahu Tongariki (1993–1995). To date a total of 890 moai statues have been recorded in topographic maps and documented by Vargas Casanova and Cristino, recording all statues present in the areas covered by the survey that comprises almost 85 percent of the surface of the island.[6] Based on these results, it is reasonable to estimate that around one thousand stone statues were carved on the island as a whole.

Several observations grew logically out of the archaeological survey and the Easter Island Statuary Project. These deal with geographic locations, forms, positions, material, shapes, sizes, and distribution of the statues. The following are the basic findings of these studies.[7]

1. The prehistoric inhabitants found in the volcanic tuffs of Rano Raraku the most suitable material to develop the monumental statuary complex that characterizes Easter Island. Almost 95 percent of the recorded statues came from this site, while only 47 statues are known to have been carved in other materials—19 in red scoria, 20 in trachite, and 8 in basalt.

2. The study of the form, structure, and stylistic attributes may be taken metrically and illustrated graphically to completely describe statue variation within the entire body of work. Positioning and proportions of design details have been determined to be uniformly symmetrical. The lack of symmetry

Figure 5.3. Partially buried moai figures at the foot of Rano Raraku's quarry. After the disappearance of the vegetation due to a sudden accumulation of loose soil from the carving of hundreds of statues, only a third of each figure is now above ground.

Figure 5.4. Moai figures, now finished, that were abandoned while being marched down the slope from the Rano Raraku quarry. Note the level of detail in the carving of the nose and the sharp shadow of the chin.

in such details as eyes, ears, and hands is insignificant. Therefore, methodological adjustments can be made in the sense that some statues, which are partially buried or otherwise inaccessible, can be measured and described on the axis.

3. It has been established that the largest number of statues are located in the south coastal zone, suggesting a significant population density for that area.

4. There are four general locations in which moai statues are to be found: quarries, mainly at Rano Raraku; in transport; on ahu; and intermediate (i.e., neither ahu nor quarry). Statues in the quarries and those in transport uniformly lack carved eye sockets, while statues with rounded and shaped eye sockets are found on or in close proximity to the ahu platforms.

5. Three hundred ninety-seven statues are still in situ at Rano Raraku quarry and the plains in its immediate environs, beautifully illustrating the different stages of the carving process. Of these, 248 are found on or are directly associated with quarries and are distributed on both the exterior and interior sides of the volcano as well as along the ridge of the local crater rim. Forty-six are located on the interior slopes of the crater and 103 on the exterior slopes. Exclusive of Rano Raraku, only 6 statues were found on quarries at different locations throughout the island.[8]

The category "in transport," is defined as statuary located between Rano Raraku quarries and any given ahu, uniformly lacking carved eye sockets. In the early stages of the statuary project, several ancient roads with statues in transport, leading from Rano Raraku to the coastal areas, were identified and plotted in topographic maps.[9] Statues in transport number 92 (11 percent) of all known sculptures. Forty-five of these are at the foot of Rano Raraku's slopes.

A total of 303 statues were found directly associated with the ahu platforms. Historically these monumental structures have been the main focus of the great majority of the inventories and research projects carried out since the late nineteenth century. All these studies have contributed useful classifications and typology, detailed metric and descriptive information on basic forms, and probable function and temporal sequence, which to a great extent have been integrated into the overall archaeological survey data.

Statues recorded in "intermediate" locations total 85. Intermediate is defined as meeting one of three criteria: (1) the sculpture arrived at the ahu, but was never erected; (2) it was erected and moved away from the ahu and re-utilized; or (3) it was erected and moved from the ahu to other locations during historic times.

6. Height is a major form variable in statues carved of Rano Raraku tuff, ranging from small figures that measure almost 40 inches to the giant statues found at the quarries that are 30 to 70 feet tall. Several types can be defined on statues of this material.

7. Statues carved in other materials are much smaller. All trachite and basalt statues are less than 6.56 feet long. Some basalt statues are truncated busts with flat rectangular faces and have bodies with rounded rectangular cross sections. Others are small portable statues 1 to 40 inches in height, found associated with inland habitation sites with rectangular houses on the southeast slopes of Maunga Tere Vaka. In several locations there are small quarries on flat basalt outcrops where these types of figures are found in different stages of carving, associated sometimes with similar anthropomorphic petroglyphs. Trachite statues were carved in local quarries at Poike and, with the exception of two examples that were transported to Hanga Roa village in historic times, all the documented figures were found associated with ahu platforms. Some of the red scoria statues are larger: four measure between 6 feet and 8 feet 2 inches long. The largest, a pillar-like figure associated with the ceremonial complex of Vinapu, is just under 11.5 feet long. With the exception of this figure, none of these statues were found associated with ahu. Two examples were found in the process of being carved in a small quarry located on the slopes of Maunga O'Tuu.

8. In terms of size, those statues that exhibit the greatest proportionate height increase are located in Rano Raraku.

In the exterior quarries, only a small number of statues are less than 9 feet long; twenty statues measure between 26 and 46 feet, while the largest measure almost 70 feet. The largest examples in the interior quarries are 29 to 30 feet. The statues in the upper quarries range from 10 to 16 feet.

The majority of the statues in transport are between 16 and 39 feet in height. Statues on ahu are consistently smaller than the majority of those in transport and measure less than 19.5 feet, with the most frequent length between 6.5 and 13 feet. Statues measuring between 19 and 23 feet are uncommon. The largest statues on ahu are: one at Ahu Hanga Te Tenga on the south coast, measuring almost 33 feet, probably broken in the process of being erected on top of the platform, and Moai Paro, resting face down at Ahu Te Pito Kura on the north coast, a statue 32.2 feet high and an estimated weight of over one hundred tons—the largest statue ever erected on top of an ahu platform.

9. Pukao, the cylindrical red scoria topknots, have been determined to be only associated with statues on ahu at the ceremonial centers of the most important lineages of the island.

PRELIMINARY ANALYSIS AND INTERPRETATIONS

A classification of Easter Island statuary has been developed based upon basic size, shape, and proportion of head and body.

The available data strongly indicate that a process of stylization took place as the statues increased in size through time. It is also evident that architectural changes occurred on ahu, associated with their statuary requirements.

A preliminary study of the statuary in its archaeological context has produced a tentative chronological ordering of types, evolving from the early, small, and more naturalistic statue form into the later large and stylized figures found at Rano Raraku and in transport.

The evidence at numerous coastal ahu supports this interpretation in the presence of several statues or statue fragments incorporated into platform masonry. All these statues are consistently smaller than those that are associated with the last construction phases of the ahu. Akahanga, a large and complex ahu site with several construction phases, provides an excellent example of reutilized statuary in ahu building and also presents a superposition of three platforms with different statue types that clearly indicates a sequence where the smaller statues are associated with the earliest platform.

While this sequence is evident in the largest and most complex ceremonial centers of the leading lineages of each territory, there is also an obvious contemporaneous variation of statue form and style in other ahu sites. The evidence at Rano Raraku quarries also supports this interpretation in the large number of statues which vary in size and are found in different stages of completion, apparently being carved at the same time.

The construction of an ahu platform, the remodeling of it to support larger statues, and the whole process of carving a statue, transporting it, and raising it on an ahu, undoubtedly required increasingly higher energy input in time and workers as the importance of image ahu as ritual centers increased. The construction of these ceremonial structures depended necessarily on the local capacities of the different family groups to successfully manage their environment and produce enough resources to support these workers. Therefore, architectural variation related to presence of decorative features, quality of construction, remodeling of structures, number, and size of statues depended on the possibilities of a social group to support a greater number of workers. Thus, differences in size of ritual centers may have resulted from intertribal competition to increase ahu and statue size as symbols of power and notable differences in size and resources of social groups."[10]

It's spectacular even today to see almost four hundred sculptures in various phases of completion in the quarries at Rano Raraku. We find them in all positions—horizontal, vertical, some in the most inaccessible places, and in numbers that suggest it would have been difficult to produce them all at once. Yet Thor Heyerdahl suggests that "an average statue of fifteen feet would take six men about a year to complete and that each sculptor had a series of statues on which to work each day. A couple of hundred men could easily keep production going even on such a grand scale."[11]

The stone carvers were skilled members of an elite guild that commanded great respect in the tribe, according to Métraux. They worked under a master and were paid in fish, lobsters, and eels. The profession was transmitted from father to son.[12]

From an examination of the statues in their various phases of completion in Rano Raraku, it is easy to determine the stages of production. After selecting an area of stone suitable for carving and, in most cases, hewing out a rectangular block, the sculptors first carved the face, next the body and hands, and then the sides. At this stage, the back of the statue was undercut from both sides to form a long keel (see figure 5.6). Then, sections of it were removed and, after placing stones beneath the statue for support, the sculptors totally cut away the keel. It was also not uncommon to carve a statue directly into the rock without first carving out a block. They used stone mallets made of lapilli, called *toki*, for carving, and most probably they were intermittently wetting the stone surface with water from a scooped-out gourd (a calabash) to soften it and control the spray of splinters. The back was carved after the statue had been moved from the quarry to the foot of the volcano slopes. The eye sockets were carved at the ahu and white coral eyes with red scoria or black obsidian pupils were inserted in them when the statue was mounted on the ahu, its final resting place. There the blind stone men were then given life the moment their eyes were set in place.[13]

How the moai statues were transported is uncertain. More than three hundred statues were moved from the quarry at Rano Raraku by means of ropes and wood poles. They were moved on ceremonial roads (*ara*), ancient paths built with compacted dirt mixed with gravel (*kikiri*) traversing several miles over rough and hilly terrain. Sections of some of these, ten to fifteen feet wide, are still visible today.[14]

Several conjectural transport methods have been suggested and some have been tested in experiments carried out on Easter Island and in other places in the world. Since 1957, original statues and replicas have been moved in vertical or horizontal positions, face up or face down, using manpower, ropes, wooden sledges, and rollers.

Oral traditions tell us that moai statues were commanded to "walk" several miles to their ahu, moved by mana, a supernatural force that certain privileged Rapanui men or women possessed. Routledge recorded from her informants that "there was a certain old woman who lived at the southern corner of the mountain and filled the position of cook to the image makers. She was the most important person of the establishment and moved the images by supernatural powers (mana), ordering them about at her will."[15] Thor Heyerdahl, during his first visit to Easter Island heading the Norwegian Archaeological Expedition in 1956, orchestrated an experiment at Anakena, where an original moai with an estimated weight of ten to fourteen tons was moved, tied on its back to a wooden sledge made from a tree fork. Over one hundred islanders pulled the statue using two parallel ropes tied to each side.[16]

Two decades later, William Mulloy theorized a method involving the use of V-shaped legs attached by ropes to the statue's neck, and a Y-shaped sledge tied to the front. In his opinion a large statue could have been transported several miles from the quarry to its ahu on the coast, moving legs forward in a bipedal fashion, with the moai hanging face down, using the protruding belly of the statue as a fulcrum.[17]

In the 1980s, two experiments carried out with concrete replicas in distant localities of the northern hemisphere proved that moai statues, at least some of them, probably could have been transported in a vertical position.

In Wyoming, Charles Love proved his conjectural method by moving a thirteen-foot, ten-ton concrete statue replica 150 feet in an upright position on top of wooden sledges running atop log rollers.[18] Almost at the same time in Strakonice, Czechoslovakia, Pavel Pavel proved his transport theory by swiveling and rocking a fifteen-foot and twelve-ton concrete moai replica in an upright position.[19]

In 1986, Thor Heyerdahl and Pavel Pavel, sponsored by the Kon Tiki Museum, tried Pavel's method in Easter Island with an original moai located close to Ahu Tongariki. Using one rope around the forehead of the statue and another around the base, they "walked" the statue. Though the experiment proved that the stability of the statue allowed moving the moai over six feet, it also proved that swiveling and rocking the statue was damaging the base, and the testing was stopped.[20]

In the late 1990s, NOVA (PBS) sponsored archaeologists Jo Ann Van Tilburg and Claudio Cristino, with a seventy-five-person crew, in an experiment to unravel how moai statues were transported and erected. Van Tilburg theorized and proved that a concrete replica of an average moai (thirteen feet high)

Figure 5.5. A profile of a moai carved out of the stone of Rano Raraku by Rapanui people (local natives only) in an experiment conducted during the Norwegian expedition lead by Heyerdahl in 1956 to estimate the amount of time required to carve one statue.

Figure 5.6. Two moai at different stages of production. Note on the right the keel is still attached to the back of the figure.

Figure 5.7. A section of the exterior quarries at Rano Raraku volcano. At the right side the largest statue ever carved, measuring seventy-one feet long, rests supine with the back still attached to the mother rock in the quarry.

could be moved horizontally in a supine position (face up), tied on a wooden sledge on top of log rollers. However, the team faced serious difficulties with the log rollers when moving the sledge. Cristino agreed that statues were moved horizontally, but in his opinion this was done with the moai face down on a sledge as the statue had to be in that position to be erected on top of the platform. Through experiments he proved statues could be moved face down and head first on a wooden sledge sliding on top of a prepared track of logs fixed and following the contour of the terrain. Once the statue arrived at the ahu, the sledge would be turned around so the statue base approached the platform first.[21]

In Vargas Casanova's opinion, though, it is possible that certain moai could have been transported by "walking" them to the ahu as some researchers and oral tradition postulate. However, this should have been on top of a wooden base to prevent damage and erosion of the base of the statue as the experiment by Pavel on a real moai proved it occurred. It is unlikely that this was the primary method used by Easter Islanders since the statues that were moved out from the quarries ranged from three to thirty feet high, and some are slender and fragile while others are thick and heavy. Thus, according to size, shape, and weight variation, as well as distance and condition of the terrain from the quarries to the ahu, Vargas Casanova postulates there must have been several ways that logs, ropes, and manpower were used to transport the statues.

Upon arrival at the ahu, their final destination, the statues then had to be mounted atop the platforms—still another feat of amazing balance and engineering increasing through time as statues grew larger.

Thor Heyerdahl hypothesized, after observing an experiment he orchestrated in Anakena in 1957, that the ancient islanders accomplished this by first moving the statue into a prone position directly in front of the altar, then levering up one side with a pole, inserting stones to keep the elevation on that side, then levering up the other side, inserting stones as a wedge, and so forth, repeating the process until the statue rested on a platform of stones the height of the altar. At that point, the statue was levered up head first in the same manner until it stood upright on the platform. He estimated that the process took twelve days to complete.[22] However, a similar procedure was followed by the

Figure 5.8. Moai figures that were ready for transport but were left at the foot of the quarry.

team of archaeologists and the Rapanui crew during the Nova experiment and it took them only a few days.

Vargas Casanova suggests another way the statues, using a ramp, were placed on the altar and then placed in a vertical position. Her theory is based on finding a stone ramp (an inclined plane) at Akahanga with an overturned moai statue resting by its side. This moai rests in an awkward position, on its own side at an odd angle, most probably the result of an accident during its erection, and this accident gave the clue. The ramp is still used today and was used in most ancient societies to facilitate the moving of heavy objects up heights.

Vargas Casanova postulates that normally, when the ahu platform was under construction, a stone ramp was built approaching the ahu platform. The statue, lying flat on a sled, was then pulled over the levered surface of the ramp using the mechanical advantage of the inclined plane and was carefully slid down to its pedestal atop of the platform when its construction was finished.

In the case of the ramp found at Akahanga, with its toppled moai nearby—probably the result of an accident—the moai may have been too close to the right edge of the ramp and slid and rotated off the ramp to the position in which we find it today (see Figure 5.10).

If they had not lost control of the statue, Vargas Casanova postulates that the following system would have been used to place the moai in a vertical position on top of the platform. First the statue, lying flat on a sled in a prone position and face down with the base toward the sea, would have been dragged on top of the ramp; then, by adding more stones gradually to the inclined plane, the moai would have been moved closer to the platform, extending the ramp so that eventually the statue would slide down to sit on the pedestal's top. Next, by adding more stones under its head, the statue would have been manipulated into an upright, vertical position, and the sled removed.

To give you an idea of the accelerating competitiveness among the Easter Island clans, we found one statue resting supine in the quarry, apparently finished but with its mother rock still attached to its back.

Figure 5.9. This construction ramp, never removed at Akahanga, was probably used to raise statues to the top of their pedestal by sliding them in a flat position.

Figure 5.10. An ahu, moai, and ramp at Akahanga, probably the remains of an accident. Here the abandoned moai most likely slid off the construction ramp, twisting as it fell into its present prostrate position.

Weighing 250–300 tons and measuring 71 feet long, it is so gigantic that some researchers think it might never have been intended to be moved. Statues within the quarry were completed except for the eyes, which presumably gave the statue its life and supernatural power. It is obvious that the power derived from these statues dominated the life of the people. Power was received after the eye sockets were carved when statues were erected on top of their ahu platforms and lost when they were toppled down and destroyed. Inlaid eyes, thoughtful and somber, carved in white pieces of coral with pupils of dark stone were set in deeply shadowed sockets. Oral traditions tell us that a statue's eyes were the entryway to the spirit, and that only after the eyes had been completed did a statue have power. According to early informants, each had a name.[23]

The phenomenon of bringing life and, thereby, power to the inert statues by inserting relatively realistic eyes is easy for even the most casual observer to see. Most early civilizations understood and used this concept. For example, the ancient Egyptians used similar bright-white eyes with black pupils, surrounded by black eye liner, to give life to their wood sculptures. The Egyptians' most ubiquitous emblem was the Eye of Horus, which symbolized healing, wholeness, strength, and perfection.[24] The Egyptians carved sculptures in relief and then painted them, emphasizing the eyes. To destroy an opposing god or king, their enemies would merely have to chisel away the eyes from a wall mural or stone relief to take away its life and power.

On Easter Island, when the villagers looked at their ancestral moai, whose presence dominated each village, they would naturally look first at their bright, piercing eyes and, conversely, they would see that their ancestors would be looking back at them—their power and presence constantly felt.

The original colors of the ancestral sculptural assemblage must have been beautiful to see in the bright subtropical sun, against the blue sky. The ahu was a colorful composition of white, yellow, and red. Its facing basalt slabs were dark gray, the fresh moai stone was yellow, and the moai's headress topknots were red, as were the horizontal bands of stone on some of the ahus' facing walls. The palette finished with bright-white coral eyes with pupils of red scoria or black stone placed into their sockets after the statues were in place.

DESTRUCTION OF THE IMAGES

During the period of upheaval after the Golden Age, the victorious party of intertribal warfare often toppled the statues of the defeated. This activity began before the arrival of the first European explorers, since early explorers discovered some statues standing and some overturned. Each subsequent explorer found more and more toppled statues until no statues were observed standing. By examining the accounts of the successive explorers, we can ascertain that the last standing statues were dismounted

Figure 5.11. Finished moai figures ready for transport. Their eyes were not carved until they were erected on their respective ahu.

shortly before 1838. We know for sure that the statues were toppled by man. Oral accounts indicate they were pulled over with ropes or undermined by removing the slab on which they rested, and onsite evidence supports these accounts.

Underlying these acts of destruction was perhaps the notion that a tribe's power was derived from its statues as they stood overlooking the elites' village. Destroying or tearing down a village's images could diminish that power. Originally the clans' competitiveness drove them to create and amass larger and larger statues, but that competitiveness later asserted itself again in acts of destruction.

Since a clan could no longer build a bigger statue to show its might, it resorted to knocking down those of its neighbors, demonstrating its power while demoralizing its neighbors at the same time, an effect more devastating than killing the villagers themselves.

The fact that all the statues in and around the quarry were left standing and were not destroyed during the time of intertribal war suggests it was undisputed neutral territory. All the statues elsewhere on the island were eventually tipped over.

STONE CROWNS OR HATS

Some of the giant statues were surmounted with stone crowns or hats (*hau*), a large cylindrical object of red scoria that came from Puna Pau, a different quarry than the one used for the large sculptures. Weighing up to twelve tons, they represented hats or the headdress (or "topknot") commonly worn on Easter Island and observed by the early European explorers. These topknot stones, known as pukao (or *hau hitirau*), were slightly hollowed out at the base to fit on the head of the stone image. This depression was not in the center, causing the brim of the hat to project forward, giving protection to the eyes of the figure, a practice also common in the native headdress. These stone cylinders were from four to eight-and-a-half feet high and six to almost ten feet in diameter. They left the quarry in a rough form. Final details and the superior knot that some had were carved at the ahu plaza. Notably, pukao are found in exclusive association with statues on ahu, never at the quarries of Rano Raraku, nor with the statues found along the ancient roads. In *The Art of Easter Island*, Heyerdahl states, "A clear

Figure 5.12. Ahu Vai Uri. Part of the Tahai ceremonial complex on the west coast. This stone-paved ramp gives access to the sea and is defined by a well-built, stepped retaining wall supporting the ceremonial plaza beyond.

Figure 5.13. Moai statues with red scoria topknots (pukao) at Ahu Nau Nau, Anakena. Variations in shape of these features suggest different functions or symbolic meaning, or may have served to indicate different lineages.

Figure 5.14 The giant images were overthrown and their ahu destroyed during the time of tribal warfare. During the eighteenth century, according to accounts of early voyages, many statues were still in place; by the nineteenth century not one was standing.

distinguishing mark of most Middle Period statues is that the apex of the head is truncated to be able to support a superimposed pukao or 'topknot.' The idea of super imposing extra 'topknots' was probably born well into the Middle Period since, at the time work was interrupted, many 'topknots' were abandoned during transportation to the ahu images that had not received any when they were originally erected." [25]

Early explorers observed that some of the islanders had red hair, a feature apparently held in high regard. Thus, the statues adorned with red topknots may represent ancestors of a special lineage or privileged status. Accounts of the first explorers tell us that the natives seemed to be obsessed by hats, stealing them from the European visitors whenever they could.

FEATHER HEADDRESSES

Easter Island natives wore hats, often decorated with special arrangements of feathers, denoting their rank or their present emotional state. They also wore special hats for festive occasions. Métraux mentions that in 1774 Forster noticed feather headdresses were not all alike and distinguished two kinds: "Many of the men wore a ring about two inches thick, plaited of grass and sitting close round the head. This was covered with great quantities of the long black feathers which decorated the neck of the man of war . . . and still others wore a simple hoop of wood, round, from which a number of the long white feathers of a gannet hung nodding and waved in the wind." [26]

According to Métraux, "The feather headdresses of Easter Island preserved in European and American museums are of four types—circlets, diadems, crescents, and conical caps." [27]

Métraux also reports that Geiseler and Thomson recorded the names of ten of the old circlets and some information concerning their special uses:

Hau hiehie were circlets made of five or six superimposed coils to which feathers from the wings and tails of black hens were fastened. . . . These large and heavy headdresses were worn by chiefs at feasts and were insignia of high office. Often they were kept in place by a strap of tapa cloth under the chin.

Hau kurakura were small crowns of variegated feathers from the cock's neck, principally the red (*kura*) feathers. These were worn by warriors in time of war. Such feathers fluttered and gave "a very warlike appearance to the warriors when they ran or danced." [28]

Hau peu-teu-ki were headdresses "of long, black, green, and variegated feathers worn by dancing people."

The *hau tara* was a "small headdress of trimmed feathers ornamented by long tail feathers used by chiefs on occasion of ceremony." [29]

Métraux also identifies other types of headdresses and distinguishes the different occasions in which these were used:

The *hau vaero* was made of long cock feathers and was "used in dancing and formerly at marriage feasts." [30]

The *hau pinei* had short black feathers.

The *hau koiro* had long, straight, projecting feathers, and was the insignia of the leading dancers.

The *hauteatea* (white headdress) was made from the feathers of white cocks which are said to have appeared on the island during the time of King Rokoroko-hetau [nineteenth century].

The *hau veri* is supposed to have been the headdress of the king.

Teketeke was the name given to the short, trimmed feathers of a circlet, as opposed to the long, projecting feathers in front. When a man was enraged against another or wanted to avenge

Figure 5.15. Warrior's feather headdress (hau kurakura) from the Smithsonian Institution Collection, Washington, D.C. Cat. #E129749–0.

Figure 5.16. Native Long-Ears portraits, one with beard and crown with feathers and one with a strange hat, which were drawn during Captain Cook's visit in 1774. Drawn from Heyerdahl, *The Art of Easter Island*, 1:39.

himself for some grave injury he turned his headdress and wore the short trimmed feathers in front. The circlets of short black feathers were also called *hau teketeke*. [31]

It is noteworthy that differences in headdresses' shapes, lengths, and the colors or arrangement of the feathers indicated different functions and symbolic meanings of these features. The same may be the case with the variations in shape observed among the statues' stone hats.

Routledge also commented concerning the customary dress and the feathered headgear:

The sole form of dress was the cloth made from the paper mulberry, and known throughout the South Seas as tapa; it was used as loin-cloths and wraps, which the Spaniards described as fastening over one shoulder. Headgear was a very important point, as witnessed by the way the islanders always stole the caps of the various European sailors. The natives had various forms of crowns made of feathers, some of them reserved for special occasions. Cherished feathers, particularly those of white cocks, were brought out

of gourds, where they had been carefully kept, to manufacture specimens for the expeditions. The crowns are generally made to form a shade over the eyes, like the headdresses of the images. [32]

PETROGLYPHS

Petroglyphs—pictorial carvings on stone—were another art form with hundreds of examples found scattered throughout the island. The petroglyphs are executed mostly in low relief, except for those at Orongo, depicting fantastic birdmen, birds, and sea creatures, but rarely humans.

One of the most spectacular and beautiful concentrations of petroglyphs on the island is carved on the rocks at the extreme end of the village of Orongo at the summit of Rano Kau volcano. Here basalt rocks jut out along the east ridge that faces the three offshore islands that were part of the Birdman Cult.

They show a fantasy Birdman with the head of a frigate bird and with a curved beak and pouch on the top of a crouching human figure. These images, mostly in profile, in a few cases that are very well preserved, clearly show the Birdman holding an egg.

Figure 5.17. At the extreme end of the village of Orongo, petroglyphs carved on the rocks represent a fantastic birdman with the head of a frigate bird and the body of a crouching human.

Figure 5.18. Petroglyph carved on a rectangular block of the upper row of the seaside wall of Ahu Nau Nau at Anakena. It is an anthropomorphic figure commonly interpreted as a lizard-man.

Figure 5.19. Detail of petroglyphs overlooking the three Birdman Cult islands.

Figure 5.20. Petroglyphs depicting two human figures on one basal block of Ahu Nau Nau's rear wall (seaside) at Anakena. They are not visible today as this wall is almost completely covered by a sand dune.

Figure 5.21. Rock at Orongo deeply carved with the figure of a Birdman.

Figure 5.22. Inspired by ancient motifs, a young islander recreates today the practice of body painting during the 2006 Tapati summer festival.

BODY PAINTING AND TATTOOING

In addition to the super sculptures, petroglyphs, and feathered headdresses, the islanders had other art forms. The most pervasive and personal was body painting. The natives looked at body painting as a form of cosmetics to enhance their beauty. They used this "makeup" of various colors, including white, red, yellow, and black—derived from mineral products and plants—to adorn their bodies before festivals, wars, dances, and ceremonial activities.

Routledge said, concerning painting:

The islanders adorn themselves with various colors: white and red were obtained from mineral products found in certain places; yellow from a plant known as "*pua*," and black from ashes of sugar cane. They had a distinct feeling for art. Some of the paintings found in caves and houses are obviously recent, and is a frequent answer to questions as to the why and wherefore of things, that they were to make some objects "look nice."[33]

Métraux also commented on this practice:

Until very recent times many women smeared their faces and bodies with red, yellow, white, and dark dyes. The red dye (*kiea*) is a red-brown, weathered and mineralized tuff, which is found in several places on the island, especially on the western slope of Poike Peninsula. Kiea was pulverized in a small stone mortar. Whole specimens or fragments of these mortars have been picked up in ancient settlements, with traces of red ochre in the hollow. . . . Another earth, probably unoxidized tuff, gives a chalk-white color (*marikuru*).[34]

Similarly, tattooing was practiced until shortly after the arrival of Christian missionaries. Here this universal practice became a fine art form in which the designs had amazing regularity and accuracy. The designs were based on geometric forms, pictures of everyday objects, and even depictions of human faces. Women were often tattooed to look as if they wore breeches, according to an account by Beechey in 1825. Under the supervision of experts (*takona*), a small bone with tiny prongs was dipped in dark color pigments and driven into the skin. This painful process was repeated many times during one's life. Routledge went on to say, concerning the art of tattooing:

Tattooing was a universal practice, and the exactness of the designs excited the admiration of the early voyagers, who wondered how savages manage to achieve such regularity and accuracy.

The drawings made for us from the descriptions of the old people show the man covered, not only with geometric designs, with pictures of everyday objects, such as chisels and fishhooks; even houses, boats, and chickens were represented in this way according to taste. The most striking objects were drawings of heads, one on each side of the body, known as "*paré-pu*," which the old mariners describe as "fearsome monstrosities." Various old persons said that they remember seeing men with a pattern on the back similar to the rings and girdle of the images.[35]

Métraux says there were two tattooed persons still living on Easter Island in 1934:

> Old Viriamo, Tepano's mother and Ana Eva Hei, the wife of Atamu Te Kena, one of the last "kings" of Easter Island. Viriamo has tights tattooed entirely of blue. Ana Eva Hei has two parallel stripes crossing her forehead from one ear to the other and the inner edge of the ear tattooed. The design on her lower jaw is composed of a triangular figure, which meets an oval design, together forming an open angle. Her hands are covered with thin blue lines reminiscent of mittens. Neither woman is completely tattooed. Viriamo refused to submit to further sittings after the tights were covered with tattooing because the operation was too painful. Ana Eva Hei, who is younger, was probably decorated when the last experts were dying.[36]

Metraux further comments on tattooing:

> Tattooing is mentioned by nearly every voyager who touches at Easter Island. Though there were probably differences between motifs used by men and by women, the features noticed by early observers are common to both. There is no way of determining the variations in design for the two sexes. . . .
>
> These variations in the extent of the tattooing surfaces are good evidence that on Easter Island as in the Marquesas, tattooing was a lengthy process that took place at different periods of life.[37]

PAINTING

The painting of the interior of stone houses and caves was an art form that included the depiction of dancing paddles, human faces, gods, birdmen, and birds. The predominant colors were red, black, white, and yellow. In addition to the prehistoric motifs, a favorite design was the European sailing ships, indicating that this art form was flourishing in the nineteenth century. The paintings were often placed opposite the entrance to the house so they could be illuminated by the daylight coming in from the entranceway. Some of these paintings were found on the walls of caves, which indicates that the art of painting was used as a decorative motif to enhance the enjoyment of what would be otherwise a dull stone environment.

Métraux, when discussing wall paintings at Orongo, states, "Several paintings at Orongo, copied by Geiseler in 1884, represent dancing paddles (*ao*) with a conventionalized human face, the big-eyed god with a schematic arrangement of the organs of the face, and birdmen facing each other.[38]

CARVING OF SKULLS

Part of the magical and religious practices of the island included incised designs on the human skull, in particular on skulls of high-status members of the Miru group. This art form included depiction of everyday objects such as fish or fowl on skulls of highly respected people; these depictions were believed to hold a power that included the supernatural ability to increase the food supply and other beneficial results. Skulls of chiefs were often stolen, so it was a normal practice to keep them hidden in secret places.

Métraux discusses this practice of preserving skulls on other Polynesian islands:

> This belief in the fertilizing power of *ariki* skulls is paralleled in other parts of Polynesia. In the Marquesas the skulls of chiefs were preserved separately and were brought out for certain public activities. Such skulls were taken on fishing expeditions to ensure a good catch and to protect the fishermen from sharks. Maoris used to

place the skull or bones of their ancestors in the sweet potato fields to procure a good harvest.[39]

Routledge also commented on this practice:

On the borderline, between religion and magic, wherever, if anywhere, that line exists, was the position of the clan known as the Miru. Members of this group had, in the opinion of the islanders, the supernatural and valuable gift of being able to increase all food supplies, especially that of chickens, and this power was particularly in evidence after death. It has been known that certain skulls from Easter are marked with designs, such as the outline of a fish; these are crania or "*puoko moa*," or fowl heads, because they had, in particular, the quality of making hens lay eggs.[40]

RONGO-RONGO TABLETS

The rongo-rongo tablet was an art form, religious tradition, and a medium for the written word. These flat, highly polished slabs of hardwood bear rows of meticulously carved stick figures on either side. Shark's teeth and obsidian flakes were used to inscribe the tablets with symbols, the origins of which remain uncertain.

The lines of hieroglyphics were carved on the tablets in two ways: either with successive lines of a story carved on opposite sides of the tablet, requiring the reader to flip the tablet over after each line to read the next; or with successive lines on the same side, left to right, then left to right upside down, and so forth, requiring the reader to invert the tablet after each line to read the next. The tablets were generally kept and chanted by rongo-rongo men, learned clansmen who preserved and taught the island's lore. Sadly, the natives' ability to read their own hieroglyphics vanished in their turbulent past. On only one occasion has someone been seen reading, chanting, and flipping the tablet over and over. That occurred during the time the islanders were being returned home from Peru by way of Tahiti. We are not sure if he was reading or faking, merely reciting a chant he had learned as a child and imitating the hand movements of the rongo-rongo man.

Routledge said, under the heading of "The Script":

The tablets, known as "*kohau-rongo-rongo*," were an integral part of life on the island within the memory of man not much past middle age. . . .

The tablets were all sizes up to six feet. . . . Every clan had professors in the art who were known as rongo-rongo men (*tangata-rongo-rongo*). They had houses apart, the sites of which are shown in various localities. Here they practiced their calling, often sitting and working with their pupils in the shade of the bananas; their wives had separate establishments. In writing, the incision was made with a shark's tooth: the beginners worked on the outer sheaths of banana stems and later were promoted to use the wood known as "*toro-miro*."[41]

The fact that the Easter Islanders had a written language is remarkable considering the island's isolation from other civilizations. The development of Western civilizations, and in particular the development of a writing system to preserve its literature, depended on contact with other cultures. The Roman alphabet we use was adapted by the Romans from the Greek alphabet, which in turn had been inherited from the earlier Phoenician traders. At Easter Island, on the other hand, no such cultural exchange was present. The islanders developed spontaneously their own writing system. Spanish Commodore Don Felipe Gonzalez visited Easter Island in 1770 and proclaimed it a territory of Spain. Gonzalez observed that the population had a form of writing that the chiefs used when they signed the Island over to Spain. Whether their signatures on the declaration were merely scribbles imitating the Spanish style of writing or whether the islanders were in fact using a writing system at that time is not known, nor is it known whether the rongo-rongo tablets were in use before or after this event.

SMALL WOODCARVINGS

Small woodcarvings were an important art form on Easter Island. The most famous wood images represented emaciated or decaying human beings, according to Métraux. The natives also carved (and still do to this day) flat wooden images of thin women, double-headed images, grotesque figures of bent-over nude men, and birdmen, the latter combining a bird's head with the body of an emaciated man.

Routledge commented on these figures:

Wooden figures are said to have been made in a considerable variety of forms, some of them being in a sitting position, others with hands crossed, etc.; names were bestowed on them—twenty—one such was repeated to us. It was not found possible to ascertain exactly what they are all intended to portray, the information being somewhat confused and contradictory, but on the whole the female figures and those with ribs seem to have been considered to be supernatural beings; they are generally called aku-aku, and sometimes atua, while the others represent men. It appears probable that they were portraits, or memorials figures, some of which may have attained deification.[42]

Métraux discusses a particular type of small wood-carvings, those of the Birdman:

The image of the birdman, a being with bird head and human body, is one of the most frequently represented figures of the petroglyphs. At Orongo, the center of the cult of the bird-headed god, this image has been carved in the rocks more than 150 times. There is a strong evidence that the bird man thus disfigured symbolizes the god Makemake. On the other hand, wooden images of this god are rare. . . .

The birdman images demonstrate the extent to which the conventional motifs were imposed on all Easter Island wood carvings. The birdman in the petroglyphs have none of the features of those cut in wood.[43]

The most classic of the Easter Island wood sculptures, an emaciated male, is known as moai kava-kava. There is no similarity in any other Polynesian island to the unique moai kava-kava figures. It is thought that the images originally were connected with spirits of the dead, although this connection has long since disappeared because the images were offered as barter. Usually the natives stored the images in their houses, carefully wrapped in tapa cloth or in secret family caves.

Figure 5.23 includes a large dance paddle showing both sides of an ao, its head carved flat with highly stylized and painted designs. The eyes are gracefully rendered with obsidian centers set in, creating a piercing look. The ears have ear plugs and are beautifully carved as part of the total composition. This paddle is an example of the islanders' superior sense of design using abstract geometry, balance, simplicity, and symmetry, much like that found in some of their architecture (e.g., the boathouse and its terrace) and arts, such as their tattooing patterns.

The small male and female figures, generally twenty to thirty inches high, have prominent ribs, collar bones, shoulders, vertebrae, and pelvises, giving them an emaciated appearance (see figures 5.24a, b, c). They are often grinning with teeth showing. The tops of their heads sometimes have a low-relief glyph. Some have beards, but all have elongated ears like the large stone statues. Designs are carved on their backs, similar to those carved on the large stone statues. It is possible that woodcarvings were the primary and first art form, evolving into the carving of the large stone statues when the wood supply was exhausted.

These small statues, like the large figures, were probably part of a system of ancestor worship. These narrow pieces of wood were carved in a much neater and proportionate way than the crude sculpture of the large statues. Their style was generally uniform but the execution varied with the skill of the carver.

SMALL STONE CARVINGS

A series of small stone carvings of varying styles and designs are part of the artistic heritage of the ancient Easter Islanders. Some of these small stone statues do not have a flat base but only a pointed end, probably so they could be stuck in the ground. It is interesting to note that these small statues have a great deal more variety in design, shape, position, and size than the conventionalized large stone statues. Some of the stone houses at the village of Orongo had doorways ornamented with carved heads.

It was customary for families to have secret family

Figure 5.23. Paddle images are from the Smithsonian Institution Collection, Washington, D.C. Cat. #E129749–0.

Figures 5.24a, b, c. Three examples of carved wood faces, in high relief, from male wooden images (moai miro). The obsidian eyes bring the otherwise inanimate figure to life. Two faces have turned heads that add another layer of expression and animation. These faces are realistic and could have been portraits or memorial figures. Photos by Kenneth Treister from the collection of the Smithsonian Institution in Washington, D.C.

caves that concealed valued family possessions, often consisting of a variety of small stone sculptures. Thor Heyerdahl tells of his visit to one of these secret family caves:

> The entrances to these caves were carefully concealed, camouflaged with stones, earth, and straw. The caves hid stone sculptures of unusual style, unlike any art form seen on the island before. . . . The cave stones, hidden in secret family caves and handed down from one generation to the next, were a variety of designs. The skull was a "key" stone that gave access to the secret opening of the cave. A powder made of human bones was placed in the hole in its forehead to kill intruders by pure magic. Note also the three-masted reed boat, a slab with ideograms, a long-eared head, and a foot. I was the first outsider to see these curious cave stones, which the owners hid from other natives as well. Here are a beast with a human head; a bearded face; a mythical whale with a reed hut and a typical Easter Island earth oven on its back and six balls under its belly; a woman with a fish roped to her shoulders; and the profile of a head.[44]

Heyerdahl also told about the correlation between small stone images and small woodcarvings:

> Some carved stone heads were inserted in the masonry wall of certain of the Orongo houses, but they were too weathered to permit removal. . . . By excavating the floor of the same house, another small image was found which was equally weathered, and broken at the neck. The natives in Mataveri identified the figure as a house image of the *moai maea* type, one which was attributed certain honors at the time of the ripening of the bananas.[45]

Furthermore, "the cult of the wooden images is not supposed to be very ancient, and was only taken up after the manufacture and direct honoring of the old stone images of Rano Raraku began to cease." . . . the custom of carving smaller house images and heads from stone only developed when the larger Rano Raraku statues were no longer manufactured.[46]

Métraux states, when discussing small stone carvings under the title "Good-Luck Objects":

> The magic significance attributed by one of my informants to the signs on the tablets probably derives from the fact that the natives considered as talismans or amulets every stone with an incised figure. Numerous boulders with engraved designs on them have been found on the island. The design that is most frequently reproduced on the stones is that of the vulva, . . . Rarely the outline of a fish, a bird, a turtle, or a man is seen. The carved figures might have increased the magic power of the stones or simply distinguish them from ordinary boulders.[47]

PAINA AND KO PEKA FIGURES

One of the most unique and unusual art forms was the creation of a large figure of woven rods called a *paina*. They had a crown of seabird wings and long ears. The host of a feast would climb into and look out from within the large sculpture. Occasionally it was put up on a special spot, where, for example, a man had been killed, but the interesting point in connection with the paina is that the usual place for erection was in front of an image ahu on its landward side, and at most, or all, of the large ahu there can still be seen, in the grass and at the foot of the paved slope, the holes where the paina have stood. The rods were held in place by four long ropes, one of which passed over the ahu. The paina festivities were held in the summer and lasted from two to four days. Routledge wrote about the painas' function: "The 'paina,' which means simply picture or representation, was given by the family as a testimonial of esteem to a father, or possibly a brother, who might be either alive or dead; it was a serious matter, and the original direction for the celebration came from a supernaturally gifted individual known as an '*ivi-atua*.'"[48]

Another giant figure, called Ko Peka, was described by the early Spanish explorers as an all-white-clothed figure, which was the focal point of a circle of natives during an all-night festival on the coast near an ahu platform. Routledge describes it: "The Spanish Expedition in 1770 says that the islanders

brought down to the beach, on the day when the three crosses were set up, an idol about 11 feet high, like a 'Judas,' stuffed with straw; it was all white, and had a fringe of black hair hanging down its back. They put it up on stones and sat cross-legged around it, howling all night by the light of flares."[48] Years later, "One of the officers of the La Pérouse Expedition (1786) also described a similar figure near a platform; it was 11 feet in height, clothed in white tapa (*étoffe blanche du pays*); it had hanging round the neck a basket covered with white, and by the side of this bag the figure of a child 2 feet long."[49]

Routledge continues with another description of one of the many festivities:

> Another great festivity, given for a father either living or dead, was the "KORO." This was a house party on a very extended scale. A special dwelling made with poles and thatched was put up, and, according to accounts, which surrounded it no doubt with a halo from the past,

measured some hundreds of feet in length and 20 feet in height. An old man stated that at a celebration at which he was present there were 'a hundred guests,' . . . 'ten cooking-places' . . . these festivities . . . seem to have lasted indefinitely, going on for months, and the time was passed with various entertainments. The old people sang, the young people danced, and the host, who lived in a little house near came and looked on. On the last day there was a great feast, and the house was broken down with the aid of the carved wooden lizards, which are associated with the island.

> There was yet another entertainment which is said to have been an honour to a mother as a koro was of a father. In at least four different places on the island are to be seen a dancing-ground known as "KAUNGA." It is a narrow strip paved with pebbles, over 200 feet in length by 2 feet in width, and not unlike the paved approach to some of the ahu.[50]

These giant and heroic statues were not ordinary works of art but carved with a passion, employing sharp, striking, and stylized features that exaggerated their form, caused deep shadows, and revealed a wonderful artistry that became the carvers' cultural tradition.

Chapter 6

THE COLLAPSE: A PASSION TO SCULPT

Figure 6.1. The giant ancestral statues, silhouetted against the blue sky, mesmerized and visually dominated the lives of the populace.

LET us step back in time a thousand years, onto the shores of Easter Island. We see no natives luxuriating among the palms, but busy people—drawing, building, surveying, and exploring the quarry for stone from which to carve a giant statue. We sense strong leadership, a strong work ethic, cooperation and enthusiasm. We hear chiseling, singing, more chiseling. In the quarry, statues are released from their stone cradles to begin the procession across the island. The islanders literally walk the statues to their altars on the shore. And then one day, all activity stops. All the lapilli picks and chisels drop to the ground, never to be taken up again. Statues in various stages of completion are abandoned in the quarry, never to take their first step. Others have just begun to toddle down the hill from their volcanic nursery, never to join their siblings beside the sea. What happened?

Usually a civilization in decline does not decline overnight—it grinds to a halt over a number of years. But here, it seems there was no gradual winding down of activity, no following through with the work that remained. Some tremendous, abrupt calamity must have occurred, although no evidence bespeaks a natural disaster. Why did these people just drop their tools and simply walk away?

The amazing rise and collapse of the Easter Island civilization—truly an enigma of the ancient world—lies suspended in time and mystery. The tiny volcanic island has concealed a fantastic drama for many years, and does to this day.

Though the collapse was no doubt the result of a complex process involving many natural and cultural phenomena, it is the authors' opinion that it was the Easter Islanders' passion for sculptural art and monumental architecture and their unequalled success in these fields that was the main underlying cause of their demise.

The Easter Islanders, so talented, well organized, and keenly but compulsively driven, sculpted and built with a passion and competitiveness far exceeding the limits imposed by their scarce resources. With each generation, ahu grew longer and wider, their statues taller and stouter.

As the people delighted in the beauty and grandeur of their ancestors hewn in stone, they grew blind to their opportunities of survival and expended a disproportionate amount of manpower and resources on the creative process. Perhaps at one point equilibrium could have been maintained, a balance between their desires to sculpt and build larger altars and their society's ability to survive. Yet once that point was passed, it was too difficult to turn back and all was lost.

An old truth is that one day one has only one year to live and one day one will have only one day to live. When was that day when the wondrous culture of Easter Island had just one year before its collapse? What was the day it had only one day before it ceased to function? That day is now clouded in a deep, sad mystery.

When we attribute the collapse, in general, to the activity of excessive artistic creation and religious flowering, we must explain that this is a root and not a specific cause. Many factors contributed either directly or indirectly under the broad canopy of the overcommitment to create, to sculpt, and to build ceremonial monumental architecture.

All civilizations are holistic, and all aspects of their society are interrelated, and all segments are linked by a cause-and-effect relationship. When a society becomes frail, it is then vulnerable to a multitude of natural and manmade ills, including the escalation of war and strife, as groups compete for dwindling precious resources.

Many types of adversities can befall a fragile civilization. With a depleted forest, limited agriculture, and intermittent natural calamities such as disease, drought, rain storms, and related erosion, social tensions on Easter Island must have grown. The tradition-bound leaders were probably unable or unwilling to make adjustments to cope with these stresses. As the stresses multiplied, competition among clans became intense, and each began to impinge on the others' territories.

Jared Diamond, in his now classic book *Collapse*, reinforces this position on Easter Island's collapse:

Easter's isolation makes it the clearest example of a society that destroyed itself by overexploiting its own resources. . . . [There are] two main sets of factors behind Easter's collapse: human environmental impacts, especially deforestation and destruction of bird populations; and the political, social, and religious factors behind the impacts, such as the impossibility of emigration as an escape valve because of Easter's isolation, a focus on statue construction . . . and competition between clans and chiefs driving the erection of bigger statues requiring more wood, rope, and food.[1]

Concurrently with our (Vargas Casanova and Cristino) study of Easter Island, Treister has been studying the ancient civilization of the Maya. These pre-Columbian Mesoamericans, like the Easter Islanders, had a glorious Golden Age of creativity lasting about a thousand years. Then it, too, suddenly and mysteriously collapsed. It is our belief that the most persuasive reason underlying the Maya's collapse is parallel to that of Easter Island.

While the Easter Islanders were overwhelmed by sculpture—the passion to sculpt and their great success in fulfilling it—the Maya were overwhelmed by their great success in architecture and in city building, and by their fierce passion to build. Whereas Easter Island possessed marvelously monumental stone sculpture and ceremonial architecture, the larger civilization of the Maya had grand architecture and monumental cities. Building and rebuilding their cities ever larger became the Maya elites' all-consuming passion, a source of pride and competitiveness that eventually undermined their strength, leaving them susceptible to a multitude of other internal and natural stresses.

In a similar fashion, also without the benefit of beasts of burden, metal tools, or the wheel, the Easter Islanders' elite devoted enormous manpower to quarrying, sculpting, and transporting stone statues. The Easter Islanders denuded their forests and caused irreversible erosion of the soils with slash-and-burn agriculture, and they deforested their small island to procure wood for housing, for transporting their images, and for other domestic uses.

Figure 6.2. With the sudden collapse, moai figures are frozen in their walk to the sea.

As the building and sculpting projects grew larger and grander, more and more manpower was enlisted, all at the expense of agriculture and other necessities of survival. We know that, at one point, the majority of the population of Easter Island was somehow involved or devoted to their creative activities.

Once the point of equilibrium was passed, their basic survival was imperiled. The Maya, on one hand, retreated to the jungle, leaving their splendid cities abandoned and deserted, while, on the other hand, the Easter Islanders retreated to their caves and focused their energies on trying to survive the inter-tribal wars.

The Easter Islanders' passion for sculpture and the Mayas' passion for architecture ultimately destroyed two wondrous prehistoric cultures. What survived are the curious fossil shells—the ruins of what were once vigorous and glorious ancient civilizations.

CONCLUSION

WE'LL never know the whole truth about Easter Island. Yet by studying its architectural and archaeological remains, we can piece together the story of an immeasurably rich civilization. Despite its hostile and lonely environment, Easter Island gave birth to a unique stone architecture, a flair for organized village planning, colossal sculpture, and still undeciphered hieroglyphics—all created in relative isolation.

To achieve such success, a society needs leisure time to create its art; unique artistic skills; motivation and a competitive spirit; an organization to manage complex building activities; and, finally, an intelligent elite to lead. Clearly, the Easter Islanders had it all.

The original Easter Island immigrants probably came with the strong artistic heritage of their Polynesian culture, plus possible subsequent inspirations brought from South America to the core of central Polynesia. They adapted to their unique geography remarkably well. Owing to the progressive scarcity of wood and their difficult coast, navigation and open-sea fishing degenerated, and the natives were forced to rely on a more stable, agricultural economy. They used volcanic stone, which was plentiful, in a myriad of forms in architecture, agriculture, and the construction of communal plazas and sculpture. And they did it marvelously well.

Most civilizations are based on older or foreign precedent. But this was the exception. Here was one culture that needed no external stimuli to develop to its zenith. The giant statues exemplify unusual genius flowering in a desolate bed of stone.

It is amazing that this tiny island has so many ruins of what were once beautiful works of architecture.

This is even more remarkable when one thinks about the fact that these examples of fine stone architecture and art were not giant communal undertakings built under the leadership of a unified government like that of the Egyptians, but rather they were designed and executed by small clans for their own territories. Cooperation at the quarry and on the roads was essential, but basically the work was regionally and independently created.

It is sad that this grand collection of artistic and architectural works is in a state of ruin. Scattered stones now blend with the natural stone landscape, only hinting at their past glory and achievement. Statues are toppled and broken, the ahu ruined, small statues and wooden tablets stolen, fitted stones thrown into disarray. War and time have taken their toll.

An important observation, perhaps relevant to our own times, concerns the collapse of the Easter Island civilization. The tremendous creativity, so successful and wondrous, was ultimately fatal. How they came to fashion their monumental sculptures and the exact way they performed the feat of transporting and erecting them remains veiled in mystery, but we do know that at one point a majority of the population was devoted to this totally inspired process. Consuming their forests and neglecting their fields, the Easter Islanders sculpted more and more, bigger and bigger works, fired by their passion to sculpt, by their pride, by their competitiveness. It was only a matter of time before their world would collapse under the weight of its own glory. Perhaps there's a lesson here for us all.

Now the magnificent, brooding statues of Easter Island are silent. Easter Island's architecture is now deserted, its dark caves empty of noise or human life. But the island's fossil remains hold in their stone memories the spirit of a creative people who once embodied the vivid excitement of creativity. To have reached such heights in their Golden Age, however short and now vanished, is a wondrous thing. Easter Island's beautifully expressed architecture and art places it unequivocally among planet earth's most wondrous civilizations.

ACKNOWLEDGMENTS

We are deeply indebted to Roberto Izaurieta for his scholarly maps and illustrations for this book, which are so important to the understanding of the history of Easter Island. We are also most grateful to Ves Spindler, a scholar and editor, who has helped with every detail in its writing, editing, and composition.

We want to thank the University of Chile and its Easter Island Studies Centre for supporting our work in Rapa Nui during the past decades. Also, we give our heartfelt recognition to the late Felipe Teao, an old Rapanui who generously shared with us his invaluable knowledge of his beloved island, and our deep gratitude to the numerous contemporary Rapanui who have worked with us for so many years in the field, contributed to documents, and helped unravel Easter Island's magnificent legacy. We wish to thank John Byram, director of the University of New Mexico Press, for his lifetime interest in the field of archaeology and the world of scholarly literature. We also want to thank the many professionals at the University of New Mexico Press for their wonderful contributions to this manuscript, particularly Lila Sanchez for her beautiful graphic design. We thank Helyne Treister for her generous encouragement and guidance to one of the authors starting on a visit to Easter Island in 1980.

We particularly want to honor and express our appreciation for the extraordinary foreword written by the world-famous architect Daniel Libeskind. He showed his true genius by presenting a most moving and poetic description of the island's historic legacy. The art of creativity did not die on Easter Island.

Note: Many sites covered in this book are part of humankind's heritage, as are all sites within the national park—which includes (about a mile from the coast) what we call the ceremonial zone and a portion of the coastal plains—plus the quarry of Rano Raraku, Orongo, the seven statues of Ahu Akivi, and other isolated notable sites that have been designated as UNESCO world heritage sites since 1995.

NOTES

CHAPTER 1

1. Arne Skjølsvold, ed., "Archaeological Investigations at Anakena, Easter Island," vol. 3, The Kon Tiki Museum Occasional Papers (Oslo, Norway: Kon Tiki Museum, 1994).

2. Patricia Vargas Casanova, Claudio Cristino, and Roberto Izaurieta, *1000 años en Rapa Nui: Arqueología del asentamiento*, Inscripción No. 157.653 (Santiago de Chile: Editorial Universitaria, S.A., 2006).

3. Andreas Mieth and Hans-Rudolf Bork, "History, Origin and Extent of Soil Erosion on Easter Island (Rapa Nui)," *Catena* 63, no. 2–3 (2005): 244–60.

4. Marshall I. Weisler and Roger C. Green, "The Many Sides of Polynesian Archaeology in Reference to the Colonization Process in Southwest Polynesia," *Rapa Nui Journal* 22, no. 2 (2008), 85–86.

5. Patrick V. Kirch, "Peopling of the Pacific: A Holistic Anthropological Perspective," *Annual Review of Anthropology* 39 (2010): 131–48.

6. Vargas Casanova, Cristino, and Izaurieta, *1000 años en Rapa Nui*, 20.

7. Mieth and Bork, "History, Origin and Extent of Soil Erosion."

8. Thor Heyerdahl, *Archaeology of Easter Island* (Chicago, New York, and San Francisco: Rand McNally, 1961), 21.

9. Carl Skottsberg, *The Natural History of Juan Fernandez and Easter Island*, vol. 1, *Geography, Geology, Origin of Island Life* (Uppsala, Sweden: Almqvist & Wiksells Boktryckeri, 1920), 426.

10. Joan Wozniak, "Settlement Patterns and Subsistence on the Northwest Coast of Easter Island. A Progress Report," *Easter Island and East Polynesian Prehistory*, ed. Patricia Vargas Casanova, 178 (Santiago: Universidad de Chile, 1998).

11. Alfred Métraux, *Ethnology of Easter Island*, Bulletin 160 (Honolulu: Bernice P. Bishop Museum, 1971), 20.

CHAPTER 2

1. Katherine Routledge, *The Mystery of Easter Island: The Story of an Expedition* (London: Sifton, Praed, 1919), 225.

2. The concept of *mana* is essential to the understanding of Polynesian cosmovision. The general usage of the term mana throughout Polynesia is defined by Kirch as a "Supernatural power or efficacy, transferred from deities to the chief by virtue of his descent." Patrick V.

Kirch, *The Evolution of the Polynesian Chiefdoms* (London: Cambridge University Press, 1984), 288. In his classic analysis of Polynesian religion, Handy derives mana from the power of the gods and refers to it as "a psychic dynamism manifesting itself physically." E. S. Craighill Handy, *Polynesian Religion*, Bulletin no. 34 (Honolulu: Bernice P. Bishop Museum, 1927), 26. Though often the source of mana referred to noble birth and primogenitural status, it was also possible for commoners to appropriate mana through complex rituals and ceremonies, as it occurred in the Birdman Cult. For a general discussion on the nature, sources, characteristics, and different expressions of mana, see Bradd Shore, "Mana and Tapu," in *Developments in Polynesian Ethnology*, ed. Alan Howard and Robert Borofsky, 137–73 (Honolulu: University of Hawaii Press, 1989).

3. For more detailed information on the Birdman Cult and the ceremonial activities held at the village of Orongo, see Sebastián Englert, *La tierra de Hotu Matua'a: Historia etnología y lengua de la Isla de Pascua* (Padre Las Casas, Chile: Imprenta y editorial, San Francisco, 1948); Routledge, *The Mystery of Easter Island*, 254–68; Métraux, *Ethnology of Easter Island*, 160, 330–41; Heyerdahl, *Archaeology of Easter Island*, 221–55, 512–16.

4. Claudio Cristino, Patricia Vargas Casanova, and Roberto Izaurieta, *Archaeological Field Guide, Rapa Nui National Park* (Santiago, Chile: CONAF, World Monuments Fund, 1986), 2–3.

5. For more information on the evolution of the pre-European population and the Easter Island cultural sequence (AD 900–1900), see Vargas Casanova, Cristino, and Izaurieta, *1000 años en Rapa Nui*.

6. An historical and anthropological account of the sequence of cultural contacts on Easter Island since 1722 to the late nineteen century and their effects over the local population is presented in Claudio Cristino, Andrés Recasens, Patricia Vargas Casanova, Edmundo Edwards, et al., *Isla de Pascua: Proceso, alcances y efectos de la aculturación. Primera parte: Historia de los contactos culturales: Configuración del proceso de aculturación* (Santiago: Universidad de Chile, Instituto de Estudios Isla de Pascua, 1984), 1–53.

7. Métraux, *Ethnology of Easter Island*, 42–43; Routledge, *The Mystery of Easter Island*, 205, 208; Heyerdahl, *Archaeology of Easter Island*, 67–68.

8. Routledge, *The Mystery of Easter Island*, 206.

9. Routledge, *The Mystery of Easter Island*, 208–9; Métraux, *Ethnology of Easter Island*, 46–47; Heyerdahl, *The Art of Easter Island* (Garden City, NY: Doubleday, 1976), 46.

10. Cristino, Recasens, Vargas Casanova, Edwards, et al., *Isla de Pascua*, 12–14.

CHAPTER 3

1. Routledge, *The Mystery of Easter Island*, 222.

2. Patricia Vargas Casanova, "Rapa Nui Settlement Patterns: Types, Function and Spatial Distribution of Households Structural Components," in *Easter Island and East Polynesian Prehistory, Proceedings of the Second International Congress on Easter Island and East Polynesian Archaeology*, ed. Patricia Vargas Casanova, 111–30 (Santiago: Universidad de Chile, Instituto de Estudios Isla de Pascua,1998).

3. Vargas Casanova, "Rapa Nui Settlement Patterns," 117–18.

4. Vargas Casanova, "Rapa Nui Settlement Patterns," 119–24.

5. Vargas Casanova, "Rapa Nui Settlement Patterns," 128. For more information on excavated sites see also William Mulloy, "The Ceremonial Center of Vinapu," in *Archaeology of Easter Island: Reports of the Norwegian Archaeological Expedition to Easter Island and the East Pacific*, vol. 1, ed. Thor Heyerdahl and Edwin Ferdon Jr., School of American Research and the Museum of New Mexico Monograph 24 (Stockholm: Forum Publishing House, 1961), 93–180; Carlyle Smith, "Tuu-Ko-Ihu Village," in *Archaeology of Easter Island: Reports of the Norwegian Archaeological Expedition to Easter Island and the East Pacific*, vol. 1, 287–90; Arne Skjølsvold, "Site E-2, A Circular Stone Dwelling, Anakena," *Archaeology of Easter Island: Reports of the Norwegian Archaeological Expedition to Easter Island and the East Pacific*, 295–304; "Archaeological Investigations at Anakena," in *The Kon Tiki Museum Occasional Papers*, vol. 3, ed. A. Skjølsvold (Oslo: The Kon Tiki Museum, 1994); Claudio Cristino, Patricia Vargas Casanova, and Roberto Izaurieta, *Prospección arqueológica de la costa norte de Isla de Pascua: Cuadrángulo 33-Hanga O Teo* (Santiago: Universidad de Chile, Instituto de Estudios Isla de Pascua, 1985); Claudio Cristino, Patricia Vargas Casanova, Roberto Izaurieta, et al., *Prospección arqueológica de la costa norte de Isla de Pascua entre sectores de Hanga O Teo y Papa te Kena* (Santiago: Universidad de Chile, Instituto de Estudios Isla de Pascua, 1986); Giuseppe Orefici, Claudio Cristino, Giancarlo Ligabue, Patricia Vargas Casanova, et al., *Proyecto Hanga O Teo: Misión arqueológica chileno-italiana a Isla de Pascua* (Centro Studi e Ricerche Ligabue de Venezia, Centro Italiano Studi e Ricerche Archeologiche Precolombiane de Brescia, Instituto de Estudios Isla de Pascua, FAU, Universidad de Chile, y Museo Sebastián Englert, Isla de Pascua, 1992); Patricia Vargas Casanova, Roberto Izaurieta, Claudio Cristino, et al., *Estudios del asentamiento: prospección y excavaciones arqueológicas de sitios habitacionales*, Serie Documentos de Trabajo: Estudios del Asentamiento, Año XII, No. 2 (Santiago, Chile: Instituto de Estudios Isla de Pascua, 1992); Catherine Orliac, Michel Orliac, et al., "Arbres et arbustes de l'Ile de Pâques. Composition et évolution de la flore depuis l'arrivée des Polynésien," Rapport Intermediare Mission Archeologique à l'ile de Pâques Oct.–Nov., 1995.

6. Vargas Casanova, "Rapa Nui Settlement Patterns," 124–26.

7. Vargas Casanova, "Rapa Nui Settlement Patterns," 114–16.

CHAPTER 4

1. Routledge, *The Mystery of Easter Island*, 170.

2. Claudio Cristino, *Report on the excavations of a marae complex, Tahinu river, Upper Papeno'o Valley, Tahiti*, Inventaire Archéologique de Polynésie Francaise, Département Archéologie, Centre Polynésien des Sciences Humaines, Punaauia, Tahiti, 1990.

3. Mulloy, "The Ceremonial Center of Vinapu."

4. Heyerdahl, *Archaeology of Easter Island*, 499.

5. Ibid., 82–88, 528–30.

6. For more details on the discussion of this topic see: Vargas Casanova, Cristino, and Izaurieta, *1000 años en Rapa Nui*, 348–49; William Mulloy, "A Preliminary Culture-Historical Research Model for Easter Island," in *Las Islas Oceánicas de Chile*, vol. 1, ed. G. Echeverria and P. Arana (Santiago: Universidad de Chile, Instituto de Estudios Internacionales, 1979), 105–51; and Mulloy and Figueroa, "The A Kivi-Vai Teka Complex and Its Relationship to Easter Island Architectural Prehistory," *Honolulu: Asian and Pacific Archaeology Series*, no. 8 (Manoa, Hawaii: Social Science Research Institute, University of Hawaii, 1978), 131–38.

7. Roger C. Green, "Rapanui Origins Prior to European Contact—the View from Eastern Polynesia," in *Easter Island and East Polynesian Prehistory, Proceedings of the Second International Congress on Easter Island and East Polynesia Archaeology*, ed. Patricia Vargas Casanova (Santiago: Universidad de Chile, Instituto de Estudios Isla de Pascua, 1998), 88.

8. Vargas Casanova, Cristino, and Izaurieta, *1000 años en Rapa Nui*.

9. Green, "Rapanui Origins Prior to European Contact," 99–109.

10. Douglas Yen, "The Sweet Potato and Oceania," in the Bernice P. Bishop Museum Bulletin 236 (Honolulu: Bernice P. Bishop Museum, 1974). See also Douglas Yen, "Easter Island Agriculture in Prehistory: The Possibilities of Reconstruction," in *First International Congress Easter Island and East Polynesia*, vol. 1, ed. Claudio Cristino, Patricia Vargas Casanova, Roberto Izaurieta, and Reginald Budd, 59–81 (Santiago: Universidad de Chile, Instituto de Estudios Isla de Pascua, 1988).

11. Green, "Rapanui Origins Prior to European Contact," 99.

12. William Mulloy, *A Preliminary Report of Archaeological Field Work February–July 1968: Easter Island*, Bulletin 1 (New York: Easter Island Committee, International Fund for Monuments, 1968).

13. Claudio Cristino and Patricia Vargas Casanova, "Archaeological Excavations and Restoration of Ahu Tongariki," *Easter Island and East Polynesian Prehistory, Proceedings of the Second International Congress on Easter Island and East Polynesian Archaeology*, ed. Patricia Vargas Casanova, 153–58 (Santiago: Universidad de Chile, Instituto de Estudios Isla de Pascua, 1998).

14. Routledge, *The Mystery of Easter Island*, 170–71.

15. Ibid., 172–73.

16. Métraux, *Ethnology of Easter Island*, 287.

17. Routledge, *The Mystery of Easter Island*, 232.

18. Englert, *La tierra de Hotu Matua'a*, 84.

19. Métraux, *Ethnology of Easter Island*, 288.

20. Felipe González, *The Voyage of Captain Don Felipe González in the Ship of the San Lorenzo, with the Frigate Santa Rosalía in Company to Easter Island in 1770–71* (Cambridge: Hakluyt Society, 1908), 102.

21. Jacob Roggeveen, "Extract from the official log of the voyage . . . in so far as it relates to the discovery of Easter Island," as quoted in Heyerdahl, *Archaeology of Easter Island*, 46–47.

22. Vargas Casanova, Cristino, and Izaurieta, *1000 años en Rapa Nui*, 202–3.

23. Jean-François de Galaup La Pérouse, *A Voyage Round the World Performed in the Years 1785, 1786, 1787 and 1788*, as quoted in Heyerdahl, *Archaeology of Easter Island*, 60.

24. As quoted in Heyerdahl, *Archaeology of Easter Island*, 59–60.

25. Roggeveen, Hervé, and Loti, as quoted in Heyerdahl, *Archaeology of Easter Island*, 60–77.

26. Routledge, *The Mystery of Easter Island*, 234.

27. Ibid., 234.

28. Métraux, *Ethnology of Easter Island*, 201.

29. Ibid., 153.

30. Patricia Vargas Casanova, Claudio Cristino, Roberto Izaurieta, et al., *Prospección arqueológica: Un estudio integral; Básico para la planificación y desarrollo de Isla de Pascua; Diagnóstico, evaluación y proyecciones del recurso cultural* (Santiago: Universidad de Chile, Instituto de Estudios Isla de Pascua, Fondecyt, 1989).

31. Jared Diamond, *Collapse: How Societies Choose to Fail or Succeed* (New York: Penguin Group, 2005), 91.

32. Patricia Vargas Casanova, "Rapa Nui Settlement Patterns."

33. Heyerdahl, *Archaeology of Easter Island*, 51–55.

34. Ibid., 56–58.

CHAPTER 5

1. Heyerdahl, *The Art of Easter Island*, 249.

2. Since the late nineteenth century several studies and inventories were carried out reporting on the moai statues. While some have been systematic efforts attempting documentation of all known statues, others report on the characteristics of some statues of specific locations. For example see Wilhelm Geiseler, *Die Öster-Insel: Easter Island a Site of Prehistoric Culture in the South Sea, Report by the Captain of H. M. Gunboat "Hyena,"* 1883, Special Offprint from No. 44 of the Supplement to the official Naval Gazette, Translation to English, 1983, in the archives of the authors; William J. Thomson, "Te Pito te Henua, or Easter Island," in *Annual Report of the Board of Regents of the Smithsonian Institution, Report of the National Museum for the Year Ending June 30, 1889* (Washington, D.C.: Government Printing Office, 1891); Routledge, *The Mystery of Easter Island*, 222; Henri Lavachery, "Notes sur l'île de Pâques," *Bulletin de la Société des Américanistes de Belgique*, Août 1933, 96–100; Cornejo, H. and P. Atan, *Inventario de las estatuas de piedra llamadas Moai*, 1935; Englert, *La tierra de Hotu Matua'a*; Arne Skjølsvold, "The Stone Statues and Quarries of Rano Raraku," in *Archaeology of Easter Island: Reports of the Norwegian Archaeological Expedition to Easter Island and the East Pacific*, vol. 1 (Santa Fe, NM: School of American Research and the Museum of New Mexico, 1961), 339–79; Vargas Casanova "Easter Island Statue Type: The Moai as Archaeological Feature," in Claudio Cristino et al., eds., *Archaeology: Proceedings of the First International Congress on Easter Island and East Polynesia, Hanga Roa, Easter Island*, vol. 1 (Santiago: Universidad de Chile, Instituto de Estudios Isla de Pascua, 1988), 131–49; Jo Anne Van Tilburg, *Power and Symbol: The Stylistic Analysis of Easter Island Monolithic Sculpture* (PhD dissertation, University of California, Los Angeles, 1986).

3. Claudio Cristino and Patricia Vargas Casanova, "Prospección Arqueológica de Isla de Pascua," *Estudios sobre la Isla de Pascua: Serie monografías anexas a los anales de la Universidad de Chile* (Santiago: Universidad de Chile, 1980), 161–62. See also: http://www.revistas.uchile.cl/index.php/ANUC/article/viewFile/23364/24701.

4. Claudio Cristino, Patricia Vargas Casanova, and Roberto Izaurieta, *Atlas arqueológico de Isla de Pascua* (*Archaeological Atlas of Easter Island*) (Santiago: Corporación Toesca 1981), plates XV–XX. After publication of this work was accomplished in 1981, field research continued, and in 1982 Jo Anne Van Tilburg (then a graduate student at UCLA) joined the Easter Island Statuary project as associated researcher, concentrating her initial work in completing documentation of statues found in Quadrants 2, 3, 5, 6, 7, and 8. Utilizing the methodology established by Vargas Casanova and Cristino of recording fifty-five discreet metric, morphological, and stylistic attributes for each sculpture documented by the archaeological survey team, a goal sought was an expansion and integration of morphological and stylistic data. Specifically, fourteen detail measurements were added, which permitted a more detailed description of such design aspects as eyes and hands, and a preliminary ordering of attributes into design categories was accomplished. An evaluation of basic field methodology during this period resulted in standardization of recording procedures allowing for the deployment of some volunteer field workers in subsequent seasons. Specially designed, large-scale measuring tools reduced the error factor to a predictable and tolerable level (two inches on major dimensions), and all data was cross-referenced and computerized. In 1983 and 1984 Van Tilburg expanded her field work to include statues documented by Vargas Casanova and Cristino in Quadrants 9, 10, 11, 12, 13, and 18 of the archaeological survey, and aspects of the unsurveyed areas. Research concerns now included details of ahu construction, examination of statue styles as related to transport techniques, reutilization of fallen statues in architecture and other forms of construction, the application of petroglyphs to statues and the significance of the use of red scoria. In 1986 Van Tilburg produced her doctoral dissertation on the stylistic analysis of 351 sculptures documented during this period.

5. Vargas Casanova, "Easter Island Statue Type." See also Vargas Casanova, Budd, Cristino, et al., *Isla de Pascua: Bases para la formulación de un programa de desarrollo: Arqueología, antropología y urbanismo* (Santiago: Universidad de Chile, 1990); Vargas Casanova, Cristino, and Izaurieta, *1000 años en Rapa Nui: Arqueología del Asentamiento* (Santiago: Editorial Universitaria, 2006), 160–68.

6. Vargas Casanova, Cristino, and Izaurieta, *Easter Island Statuary Project Thematic Map* (Santiago: University of Chile, 1987). This map included information on the distribution, material, and location of 818 moai statues recorded between 1977 and 1987. Distribution: 422 moai in 24 Quadrants and 396 within Rano Raraku Area. Material: tuff, 772; basalt, 8; red scoria, 19; trachyte, 19. Location: in quarry, 353; in transport, 92; on Ahu, 288; and intermediate location, 85). See also Vargas Casanova, "Easter Island Statue Type."

7. Basic findings of the Archaeological Survey and on the Easter Island Statuary project were presented in Vargas Casanova's paper "Easter Island Statue Type," at the First International Congress on Easter Island and East Polynesia, Hanga Roa, September 6–12, Rapa Nui, 1984. A revised version of this paper, including data of other forty-five statues collected between 1986 and 1987 was published in Cristino et al., eds., *Archaeology: Proceedings of the First International Congress on Easter Island and East Polynesia, Hanga Roa, Easter Island*, vol. 1 (Santiago: Universidad de Chile, 1988), 133–49. For more details and conclusions based on data of all recorded statues see Vargas Casanova, Cristino, and Izaurieta, *1000 años en Rapa Nui*, 160–68.

8. Originally, in the 1979–1980 field seasons, 396 moai were recorded within the Rano Raraku area. In 1993 a large statue was discovered after some excavations were practiced at the foot of the exterior Rano Raraku slopes. It was buried at a depth of three feet, face up in a horizontal position, covered by a thick layer of soil formed by the debris from the carving process of the quarries uphill. With the addition of this new moai the total number of recorded statues in the Rano Raraku area is 397. For details on this finding see "Dans la carriere du Rano Raraku: Découverte d'un nouveau Moai à l'Ile de Pâques," *La Depeche: Magazin du Grand Pacifique, Tahiti*, Lundi 22 Fevrier 1993.

9. Cristino, Vargas Casanova, and Izaurieta, *Atlas arqueológico de Isla de Pascua*; Cristino, Vargas Casanova, and Izaurieta, *Prospección arqueológica de la costa norte de Isla de Pascua: Cuadrángulo 33-Hanga O Teo*; Cristino, Vargas Casanova, Izaurieta, et al., *Prospección arqueológica de la costa norte de Isla de Pascua entre sectores de Hanga O Teo y Papa te Kena*; Vargas Casanova, "Easter Island Statue Type"; Vargas Casanova, Budd, et al., *Prospección arqueológica en el*

Faldeo Sur del Maunga Tere Vaka: Un estudio integral del asentamiento interior en altura (Santiago: Fondecyt, 1988). Vargas Casanova, Izaurieta, Budd, et al., *Estudios del asentamiento de Isla de Pascua: Prospección arqueológica de la península del Poike y Sector de Mahatua* (Santiago: Universidad de Chile, 1990); Vargas Casanova, Cristino, and Izaurieta, *1000 años en Rapa Nui*, 160–68.

10. Vargas Casanova, "Easter Island Statue Type," 146–49.

11. Heyerdahl, *The Art of Easter Island*, 157.

12. Métraux, *Ethnology of Easter Island*, 221.

13. Vargas Casanova, "Easter Island Statue Type"; Vargas Casanova, Cristino, and Izaurieta, *1000 años en Rapa Nui*.

14. Vargas Casanova, "Easter Island Statue Type"; Vargas Casanova, Cristino, and Izaurieta, *1000 años en Rapa Nui*.

15. Routledge, *The Mystery of Easter Island*.

16. Heyerdahl, *Archaeology of Easter Island*.

17. William Mulloy, "A Speculative Reconstruction of Techniques of Carving, Transporting and Erecting Easter Island Statues," *Archaeology and Physical Anthropology in Oceania* 1 (1970): 1–23.

18. Charles Love, "How to Make and Move an Easter Island Statue," in *State and Perspectives of Scientific Research in Easter Island Culture*, ed. Heide-Margaret Esen-Baur (Frankfurt: Courier Forschungs Institut Sem'kenberg 125, 1990), 139–40.

19. Pavel Pavel, "Reconstruction of the Transport of Moai," in *State and Perspectives of Scientific Research in Easter Island Culture*, ed. Heide-Margaret Esen-Baur, 141–44 (Frankfurt: Courier Forschungs Institut Sem'kenberg 125, 1990); see also: "Reconstruction of the Transport of the Moai Statues and Pukao Hats," *Rapa Nui Journal* 9 (1995): 69–72.

20. For more details about this experiment, see Heyerdahl, *Easter Island: The Mystery Solved* (New York: Random House, 1989); Vargas Casanova, field observations in report to the National Council for Monuments on the experiment carried out at Hanga Nui, Easter Island, manuscript on file with author. In 2012 another experiment conducted in Hawaii by Hunt et al. again proved that it was possible to move a concrete moai replica by swiveling and rocking the statue in vertical position. However, though it gave a most realistic impression that statues may have been "walked" to their final destination, the experiment failed to prove that moai carved out of the fragile tuff of Rano Raraku quarries could have resisted the traction of that movement, as well as the erosion that should have resulted from the direct friction of the base over the rough terrain, without serious damage to the statue. Certainly, conclusions derived from the performance of a replica made out of concrete cannot be applied to the tuff from which were carved the real moai.

21. *Secrets of Easter Island: Move a Megalith*, available online at http://www.pbs.org/wgbh/nova/easter/move.

22. Heyerdahl, *Archaeology of Easter Island*.

23. Geiseler, *Die Öster-Insel*.

24. The ancient Egyptians used similar bright-white eyes with black pupils surrounded by black eye liner in their wood sculptures to give them life. The Egyptians' most ubiquitous emblem was the Eye of Horus, which symbolized healing, wholeness, strength, and perfection.

25. Heyerdahl, *The Art of Easter Island*, 157.

26. Métraux, *Ethnology of Easter Island*, 221.

27. Ibid., 220.

28. Geiseler, *Die Öster-Insel*, 35.

29. Thomson, "Te Pito te Henua," 535.

30. John Macmillan Brown, *The Riddle of the Pacific* (London: Fisher Unwin, 1924), as cited in Métraux, *Ethnology of Easter Island*, 222–23.

31. Métraux, *Ethnology of Easter Island*, 222–23.

32. Routledge, *The Mystery of Easter Island*, 218.

33. Ibid., 220.

34. Métraux, *Ethnology of Easter Island*, 236.

35. Routledge, *The Mystery of Easter Island*, 219–20.

36. Métraux, *Ethnology of Easter Island*, 238–39.

37. Ibid., 240–41.

38. Ibid., 272.

39. Ibid., 267.

40. Routledge, *The Mystery of Easter Island*, 240.

41. Ibid., 243–44.

42. Ibid., 270–71.

43. Métraux, *Ethnology of Easter Island*, 256–57.

44. Thor Heyerdahl, *Aku-Aku: The Secret of Easter Island* (Chicago, New York, and San Francisco: Rand McNally, 1958), 304–5.

45. Heyerdahl, *Archaeology of Easter Island*, 80.

46. Ibid., 81–82.

47. Métraux, *Ethnology of Easter Island*, 263.

48. Routledge, *The Mystery of Easter Island*, 233.

49. Ibid., 233–34.

50. Ibid., 234.

CHAPTER 6

1. Diamond, *Collapse*, 118–19.

SELECTED BIBLIOGRAPHY

Anderson, Atholl. "The Ideal Free Distribution, Food Production, and the Colonization of Oceania." In *Behavioral Ecology and the Transition to Agriculture*, edited by D. J. Kennett and B. B. Winterhalder, 265–288. Berkeley: University of California Press, 2006.

———."Towards the Sharp End: The Form and Performance of Prehistoric Polynesian Voyaging Canoes." In *Pacific 2000, Proceedings of the Fifth International Conference on Easter Island and the Pacific*, edited by Cristopher M. Stevenson et al., 29–36. Los Osos, CA: Easter Island Foundation, 2001.

Ayres, William S. "The Tahai Settlement Complex." In *Archaeology: Proceedings of the First International Congress on Easter Island and East Polynesia, Hanga Roa, Easter Island*, vol. 1, edited by Claudio Cristino et al., 95–119. Santiago: Universidad de Chile, Instituto de Estudios Isla de Pascua, 1988.

Bahn, Paul, and John Flenley. *Easter Island, Earth Island*. London: Thames and Hudson, 1992.

Baker, Peter. "Petrological Factors Influencing the Utilization of Stone on Easter Island." In *Easter Island in Pacific Context. South Seas Symposium. Proceedings of the Fourth International Conference on Easter Island and East Polynesia*, edited by Christopher Stevenson, Georgia Lee, and F. J. Morin. Los Osos, CA: Easter Island Foundation, 1998.

———. "Preliminary Account of Recent Geological Investigations on Easter Island." *Geological Magazine* 104, no. 2 (1967).

Barthel, Thomas S. *The Eighth Land: The Polynesian Discovery and Settlement of Easter Island*. Honolulu: The University Press of Hawaii, 1978.

Beaglehole, J. C., ed. *The Journals of Captain James Cook on His Voyages of Discovery: The Voyage of the Resolution and Endeavor*. Cambridge: The Hakluyt Society, 1961.

Beechey, F. W. *Narrative of a Voyage to the Pacific and Beering's Strait to cooperate with the Polar expeditions performed in H. M. Ship Blossom, under the command of C.F.W. Beechey in the years 1825, 26, 27, 28*. 2 vols. London: H. Colburn and R. Bentley, 1831.

Brown, John Macmillan. *The Riddle of the Pacific*. London: Fisher Unwin, 1924.

Budd, Reginald, and Patricia Vargas Casanova. *Arquitectura prehistórica de Isla de Pascua*. Santiago: Universidad de Chile, 1993. http://www.isladepascua.uchile.cl/Publicaciones.

Bustamante, Patricio, Javier Tuki, Karlo Huke, Juan Tepano, and Rafael Tuki Tepano. *Empleo de astronomía y geometría básicas en el emplazamiento de sitios y en la división territorial durante el reinado de Hotu Matu'a en Rapa Nui*. Electronic publication edited by Patricia Vargas Casanova. http://www.isladepascua.uchile.cl.

Cook, James. *Diario de James Cook, del 17 de marzo*. 1774. http://www.CaptainCookSociety.com.

———. *A Voyage Towards the South Pole and Round the World, Performed in the Resolution and Adventure, in the years 1772, 1773, 1774, 1775*. 2 vols. London: W Strahan and T Cadell, 1777.

Cooke, George Henry, and William Edwin Safford. "Te Pito te Henua, Known as Rapa Nui; Commonly Called Easter Island, South Pacific Ocean." *Annual Report of the Board of Regents of the Smithsonian Institution*, 691–723. Washington D.C.: Smithsonian Institution, 1899.

Cristino, Claudio. *Informe preliminar de la restauración de la Aldea Ceremonial de Orongo*. Documentos de Trabajo, Año XV, Facultad de Arquitectura y Urbanismo (hereafter FAU). Santiago: Universidad de Chile, Instituto de Estudios Isla de Pascua, 1995.

———. *Proposición de una estrategia metodológica para el estudio de patrones de asentamiento*. Tesis de Grado en Antropología, Mención en Arqueología. Universidad de Chile, 1979.

———. *Report on the excavations of a marae complex, Tahinu river Upper Papeno,o Valley, Tahiti*. Inventaire Archéologique de Polynésie Francaise. Département Archéologie, Centre Polynésien des Sciences Humaines. Punaauia, Tahiti: 1990.

———. "Restauración del Centro Ceremonial de Orongo, Isla de Pascua." *AUCA* 32 (Santiago, 1977).

Cristino, Claudio, and Edmundo Edwards. Preliminary Report on the Survey and Excavations at Motu Nui and Motu Iti, Easter Island. Personal papers of the authors, Santiago, Chile, 1984.

———. "Islet Re-Visited: Survey and Excavations at the Off-Shore Islet of Motu Nui, Easter Island." Paper presented at the First International Congress on Easter Island and East Polynesia, Hanga Roa, Rapa Nui, September 6–12, 1984.

Cristino, Claudio, and Patricia Vargas Casanova. "The Easter Island Rectangular Houses Complex." Paper presented at the First International Congress on Easter Island and East Polynesia, Hanga Roa, Rapa Nui, September 6–12, 1984.

———. "Ahu Tongariki, Easter Island: Chronological and Sociopolitical Significance." *Rapa Nui Journal* 13, no. 3 (1999): 67–69.

———. "Archaeological Excavations and Reconstruction of Ahu Tongariki, Easter Island." *Revista de Urbanismo* 5 (2002): 1–10. http://www.revistas.uchile.cl/index.php/RU/article/viewArticle/12951/13235.

———. "Archaeological Excavations and Restoration of Ahu Tongariki." In *Easter Island and East Polynesian Prehistory, Proceedings of the Second International Congress on Easter Island and East Polynesia Archaeology*, edited by Patricia Vargas Casanova, 153–58. Santiago: Universidad de Chile, Instituto de Estudios Isla de Pascua, 1998.

———. "Archaeological Excavations and Restoration of Ahu Tongariki, Easter Island." Paper presented at the Second International Congress on Easter Island and Eastern Polynesian Archaeology, Santiago, Chile: Instituto de Estudios Isla de Pascua, Universidad de Chile, Hanga Roa, Rapa Nui, 17–21 October, 1996.

———. *Easter Island Archaeological Survey. Reports of Quadrants 3, 7, 14, 18, 28, 30, 31, and 33.* Unpublished manuscripts on file with authors, Santiago, Chile, written 1976–1986.

———. "Prospección Arqueológica de Isla de Pascua." *Isla de Pascua. El asentamiento interior en Altura*, edited by Patricia Vargas Casanova, 3–7. Santiago, Chile: Universidad de Chile, Instituto de Estudios Isla de Pascua, 1989.

———. "Radiocarbon Dates from Ahu Tongariki, Easter Island." Unpublished 2005 report on file with the authors, Santiago, Chile.

Cristino, Claudio, and Roberto Izaurieta. "Easter Island: Total Land Area of Te Pito o Te Henua." *Rapa Nui Journal* 20, no. 1 (2006): 81.

Cristino, Claudio, Alejandro Estrada, Roberto Izaurieta, R. Palma, and R. Morales. *Memoria en la Piedra: Contribución al estudio del arte rupestre del arte repestre en Rapa Nui.* Santiago: Universidad de Chile, Instituto de Estudios Isla de Pascua, 2006.

Cristino, Claudio, Andrés Recasens, Patricia Vargas Casanova, Edmundo Edwards, et al. *Isla de Pascua: Proceso, alcances y efectos de la aculturación.* Santiago: Universidad de Chile, Instituto de Estudios Isla de Pascua, 1984.

Cristino, Claudio, Patricia Vargas Casanova, and Roberto Izaurieta. *Archaeological Field Guide. Rapa Nui National Park.* Santiago, Chile: CONAF, World Monuments Fund, 1986.

———. *Archaelogical Field Guide. Rapa Nui National Park.* Santiago, Chile: CONAF, World Monuments Fund, 1987.

———. *Atlas arqueológico de Isla de Pascua (Archaeological Atlas of Easter Island).* Santiago, Chile: Corporación Toesca, 1981.

———. *Investigaciones y Reconstrucción de Ahu Tongariki, Isla de Pascua. Recuento Prelíminar de las excavaciones arqueológicas 1993–94.* Santiago: Universidad de Chile, Instituto de Estudios Isla de Pascua, 1994.

———. *Plano de la Prospección Arqueológica del Cuadrángulo 18 Maunga O Koro.* Santiago: Universidad de Chile, Instituto de Estudios Isla de Pascua, 1980.

———. *Plano de la Prospección Arqueológica del Sector de Vai Mata, Cuadrángulo 32.* En archivo Instituto de Estudios Isla de Pascua. Santiago: Universidad de Chile, 1985.

———. *Prospección Arqueológica de la Costa Norte de Isla de Pascua. Cuadrángulo 33-Hanga O Teo.* En archivo Instituto de Estudios Isla de Pascua. Santiago: Universidad de Chile, Instituto de Estudios Isla de Pascua, 1985.

Cristino, Claudio, and Patricia Vargas Casanova, et al. *Estudios sobre la Isla de Pascua.* Serie Monografías Anexas a los Anales de la Universidad de Chile. Santiago: Ediciones de la Universidad de Chile, 1980. http://www.revistas.uchile.cl/index.php/ANUC/article/viewFile/23364/24701

Cristino, Claudio, Patricia Vargas Casanova, Roberto Izaurieta, and Reginald Budd. *Plano de la prospección arqueológica del sector de Papa Te Kena, Cuadrángulo 34.* Santiago: Universidad de Chile, Instituto de Estudios Isla de Pascua, 1986.

Cristino, Claudio, Patricia Vargas Casanova, Roberto Izaurieta, and Reginald Budd, eds. *Archaeology: Proceedings of the First International Congress on Easter Island and East Polynesia, Hanga Roa, Easter Island*, vol. 1. Santiago: Universidad de Chile, Instituto de Estudios Isla de Pascua, 1988.

Cristino, Claudio, Patricia Vargas Casanova, Roberto Izaurieta, L. González, and Reginald Budd. *Prospección arqueológica de la costa norte de Isla de Pascua, entre sectores de Hanga O Teo y Papa te Kena.* Santiago: Universidad de Chile, Instituto de Estudios Isla de Pascua, 1986.

"Dans la carriere du Rano Raraku. Découverte d'un Nouveau Moai à l'Ile de Pâques." *La Dépêche: Magazin du Grand Pacifique.* Tahiti, Lundi 22 Fevrier 1993.

Diamond, Jared. *Collapse: How Societies Choose to Fail or Succeed.* New York: Penguin Group, 2005.

Dye, Tom, and David. W. Steadman. "Polynesian Ancestors and Their Animal World." *American Scientist* 78 (1990): 207–15.

Edwards, Edmundo, and Malcolm Clark. "Preliminary Report on Possible Astronomical Relationships in Quadrangle 31, Ahu Raai." Paper presented at the First International Congress on Easter Island and East Polynesia, Hanga Roa, Rapa Nui, September 6–12, 1984.

Edwards, Edmundo, Claudio Cristino, and Jack Grove. "El Niño (ENSO) and Its Influence on the Prehistoric Culture of Easter Island." Paper presented at the Second International Congress on Easter Island and Eastern Polynesian Archaeology, Santiago, Chile, Instituto de Estudios Isla de Pascua, Universidad de Chile, Hanga Roa, Rapa Nui, October 17–21, 1996.

Edwards, Edmundo, Claudio Cristino, Jack Grove, and Alexandra Edwards. "Application des études paléo-climatiques pour l'archéologie. Effets possibles des phénomènes 'El Niño' dans les temps anciens." *Bulletin de la Société des Études Océaniennes* (BSEO) 281/282, no. 2–11 (Juin/Septembre 1999).

Englert, Sebastián. *Island at the Center of the World: New Light on Easter Island.* Translated and edited by William Mulloy. Photos by George Holton. New York: Scribner, 1970.

———. *Primer siglo cristiano de la Isla de Pascua.* Villarrica, Chile: Escuela Lito-Tipografica Salesiana, 1964.

———. *La tierra de Hotu Matua: Historia etnología y lengua de la Isla de Pascua.* Padre Las Casas, Chile: Editorial San Francisco, 1948.

———. *Tradiciones de la isla de Pascua, en idioma rapanui y castellano, por el p. Sebastián Englert . . . .* Padre Las Casas, Chile: Editorial San Francisco, 1939.

Evans, Clifford. "The Dating of Easter Island Archaeological Obsidian Specimens." In *Archaeology of Easter Island: Reports of the Norwegian Archeological Expedition to Easter Island and the East Pacific*, vol. 2, edited by Thor Heyerdahl and Edwin Ferdon Jr. Monographs of the Kon-Tiki Museum 24. Stockholm: Kon-Tiki Museum, 1965.

Ferdon, Edwin, Jr. "A Summary of the Excavated Record of Easter Island Prehistory." In *Archaeology of Easter Island: Reports of the Norwegian Archaeological Expedition to Easter Island and the East Pacific*, vol. 1, edited by Thor Heyerdahl and Edwin Ferdon Jr., 527–35. Monographs of the School of American Research and the Museum of New Mexico 24. Stockholm: Kon-Tiki Museum, 1961.

———. "Easter Island House Types." In *Archaeology of Easter Island: Reports of the Norwegian Archaeological Expedition to Easter Island and the East Pacific*, vol. 1, edited by Thor Heyerdahl and Edwin Ferdon Jr., 329–38. Monographs of the School of American Research and the Museum of New Mexico 24. Stockholm: Kon-Tiki Museum, 1961.

Finney, Ben. "Voyaging and Isolation in Rapa Nui Prehistory." *Rapa Nui Journal* 7, no. 1 (March 1993): 1–6.

Flenley, John. "Stratigraphic Evidence of Environmental Change on Easter Island." *Asian Perspectives* 22 (1979): 33–40.

———. "The Late Quaternary Vegetational History of Easter Island." Paper presented at the First International Congress, Easter Island and East Polynesia, Hanga Roa, Rapa Nui, September 6–12, 1984.

Flenley, John, and Paul Bahn. *The Enigmas of Easter Island: Island on the Edge.* Oxford, NY: Oxford University Press, 2003.

Forster, George. *A Voyage Round the World in His Britannic Majesty's Sloop, Resolution, Commanded by Capt. James Cook, During the Years 1772, 3, 4, and 5.* 2 vols. Farmington Hills, MI: Gale ECCO, 2010/2012.

Geiseler, Wilhelm. *Die Öster-Insel: Easter Island a Site of Prehistoric Culture in the South Sea. Report by the Captain of H. M. Gunboat "Hyena," 1883.* Special Offprint from No. 44 of the Supplement to the official Naval Gazette. Translation to English, 1983, in the archives of the authors.

———. *Geiseler's Easter Island Report: An 1880s Anthropological Account.* Introduction, annotations, and notes by William S. Ayres. Translated by William S. Ayres and Gabriella S. Ayres. Honolulu: Social Science Research Institute, University of Hawaii at Manoa, 1995.

Gilbert, Joseph. "Gilbert's Account of Easter Island: Extract of the journal of the Master of the Resolution, 16 March, 1774, by H. D. Skinner." *Journal of the Polynesian Society* 28, no. 3 (1919).

Gill, W. George. *Final Report of Investigations of the 1981 Easter Island Anthropological Expedition.* Manuscript on file. Washington, D.C.: National Geographic Society, 1986.

———. "Investigations of the 1981 Easter Island Anthropological Expedition." In *Easter Island Archaeology: Research on Early Rapanui Culture*, edited by Christopher M. Stevenson and William S. Ayres. Easter Island Foundation, 2000.

Gill, George W., and D. W. Owsley. "Human Osteology of Rapa Nui." In *Easter Island Studies*, edited by S. R. Fisher. Oxford, UK: Oxford Books, 1993.

Golson, J. "Thor Heyerdahl and the Prehistory of Easter Island." *Oceania* 36 (1965).

González, Felipe. *The Voyage of Captain Don Felipe González in the Ship of the San Lorenzo, with the Frigate Santa Rosalía in company to Easter Island in 1770–71.* 2nd series, no. 13. Cambridge: Hakluyt Society, 1908.

Graves, Michael, and Roger C. Green, eds. *The Evolution and Organization of Prehistoric Society in Polynesia.* New Zealand Archaeological Association Monograph, no. 19. Auckland: New Zealand Archaeological Association, 1993.

Green, Roger C. "Community-Level Organization, Power and Elites in Polynesian Settlement Pattern Studies." In *The Evolution and Organization of Prehistoric Society in Polynesia*, edited by M. Graves and R. Green, 9–12. Auckland: New Zealand Archaeological Association, 1993.

———. "Linguistic Subgrouping Within Polynesia: The Implications for Prehistoric Settlement." *Journal of the Polynesian Society* 75 (1966): 6–38.

———. "Origins for the Rapanui of Easter Island Before European Contact: Solutions from Holistic Anthropology to an Issue No Longer Much of a Mystery." *Rapa Nui Journal* 14, no. 3 (2000): 71–76.

———. "Rapanui Origins Prior to European Contact—the View from Eastern Polynesia." In *Easter Island and East Polynesian Prehistory: Proceedings of the Second International Congress on Easter Island and East Polynesia Archaeology*, edited by Patricia Vargas Casanova, 87–110. Santiago: Universidad de Chile, Instituto de Estudios Isla de Pascua, 1998.

———. "Settlement Pattern Studies in Oceania: An Introduction to a Symposium." *New Zealand Journal of Archaeology* 6 (1984): 59–69.

———. "Subgrouping of the Easter Island Language in Polynesia and Its Implications for the East Polynesian Prehistory." In *Archaeology: Proceedings of the First International Congress on Easter Island and East Polynesia, Hanga Roa, Easter Island*, edited by Claudio Cristino et al., 35–57. Santiago: Universidad de Chile, Instituto de Estudios Isla de Pascua, 1988.

Handy, E. S. Craighill. *Polynesian Religion.* Bernice P. Bishop Museum Bulletin no. 34. Honolulu: The Bernice P. Bishop Museum, 1927.

Hather, Jon, and Patrick V. Kirch. "Prehistoric Sweet Potato (Ipomoea batatas) from Mangaia Island, Central Polynesia." *Antiquity* 65 (1991): 887–93.

Hervé, Juan. *Narrative of the Expedition Undertaken by Order of His Excellency Don Manuel de Amat, Viceroy of Peru . . . to the Island of David in 1770.* 2nd series, vol. 13. Cambridge: Hakluyt Society, 1908.

Heyerdahl, Thor. *Aku-Aku: The Secret of Easter Island.* Chicago, New York, and San Francisco: Rand McNally, 1958.

———. *Archaeology of Easter Island.* Chicago, New York, and San Francisco: Rand McNally, 1961.

———. *The Art of Easter Island.* Garden City, NY: Doubleday, 1976.

———. *Easter Island: The Mystery Solved.* New York: Random House, 1989.

Heyerdahl, Thor, and Edwin Ferdon Jr., eds. *Archaeology of Easter Island: Reports of the Norwegian Archaeological Expedition to Easter Island and the East Pacific*, vol. 1. Monographs of the School of American Research and the Museum of New Mexico 24. Stockholm: Kon-Tiki Museum, 1961.

———. "An Introduction to Easter Island." In *Archaeology of Easter Island: Reports of the Norwegian Archaeological Expedition to Easter Island and the East Pacific*, vol. 1. Monographs of the School of American Research and the Museum of New Mexico 24. Stockholm: Kon-Tiki Museum, 1961.

Hotus, Alberto, Juan Chavez, Juan Haoa, José Fati, et al. "Te Mau Hatu O Te Kainga O Te Pito O Te Henua O Rapa Nui." Paper presented at the Primer Congreso Internacional Isla de Pascua y Polinesia Oriental. Sección Antropología: Cambio Cultural en Isla de Pascua y Polinesia Oriental, 6–12. Septiembre, Hanga Roa, Rapa Nui, 1984.

———. "Te mau hatu'o Rapa Nui: Los soberanos de Rapa Nui." In *Los soberanos de Rapa Nui: Pasado, presente y futuro de Rapa Nui.* Santiago, Chile, Editorial Emisión, 1988.

Hunt, Terry, and Carl Lipo. "Late Colonization of Easter Island." *Science* 311, no. 5767 (March 17, 2006): 1603–6.

Hunter-Anderson, Rosalind L. "Human vs. Climatic Impacts at Rapa Nui: Did the People Really Cut Down All Those Trees?" *Easter Island in Pacific Context, Proceedings of the Fourth International Conference on Easter Island and East Polynesia*, edited by Christopher M. Stevenson, Georgia Lee, and F. J. Morin. Los Osos, CA: Easter Island Foundation, 1998.

Irwin, Geoffrey. *The Prehistoric Exploration and Colonisation of the Pacific.* London: Cambridge University Press, 1994.

Kirch, Patrick V. *The Evolution of the Polynesian Chiefdoms.* London: Cambridge University Press, 1984.

———. *On the Road of the Winds: An Archaeological History of the Pacific Islands Before European Contact.* Berkeley: University of California Press, 2000.

———. "Peopling of the Pacific: A Holistic Anthropological Perspective." *Annual Review of Anthropology* 39 (2010): 131–48.

———. "The Transformation of Polynesian Societies: Archaeological Issues." In *Archaeology: Proceedings of the First International Congress: Easter Island and East Polynesia, Hanga Roa, Easter Island,* vol. 1, edited by Claudio Cristino et al., 1–12. Santiago: Universidad de Chile, Instituto de Estudios Isla de Pascua, 1988.

Kirch, Patrick V., ed. "Island Societies: Archaeological Approaches to Evolution and Transformation." In *New Directions in Archaeology.* London: Cambridge University Press, 1986.

Kirch, Patrick V., John Flenley, and David W. Steadman. "A Radiocarbon Chronology for Human-Induced Environmental Change on Mangaia, Southern Cook Islands, Polynesia." *Radiocarbon* 33, 1991.

La Pérouse, Jean-François de Galaup. *A Voyage Round the World Performed in the Years 1785, 1786, 1787 and 1788.* 2 vols. and atlas. Originally edition published in Paris (1797) and London (1798).

Larenas, Felipe Andrés, and Patricia Vargas Casavova. *Estudios del asentamiento en Isla de Pascua.* Santiago: Universidad de Chile, Instituto de Estudios Isla de Pascua, 2005.

Lavachery, Henri. "Notes sur l'île de Pâques." *Bulletin de la Société des Américanistes de Belgique, Août* (1933): 96–100.

Lee, Georgia. *Easter Island Rock Art: Ideological Symbols As Evidence of Sociopolitical Change.* PhD dissertation. Los Angeles: University of California, 1986.

———. "Preface." In *Archaeological Investigations on Easter Island: Maunga Tari: An Upland Agricultural Complex,* edited by Christopher M. Stevenson and Georgia Lee, xiii. Los Osos, CA: Easter Island Foundation, 1997.

———. *The Rock Art of Easter Island: Symbols of Power, Prayers to the Gods.* Los Angeles: The Institute of Archaeology Publications, University of California, 1992.

———. "The Rock Art of Rapa Nui." Paper presented at the First International Congress, Easter Island and East Polynesia, Hanga Roa, Rapa Nui, September 6–12, 1984.

Ligabue, Giancarlo, and Giuseppe Orefici, eds. *Rapa Nui. Gli Ultimi Argonauti.* Venezia: Erizzo Editrice, 1994.

Loti, Pierre. *Isla de Pascua.* Santiago: LOM Ediciones, 1998.

Love, Charles. "How to Make and Move an Easter Island Statue." In *State and Perspectives of Scientific Research in Easter Island Culture,* edited by Heide-Margaret Esen-Baur, 139–40. Frankfurt: Courier Forschungsinstitut Senckenberg, 1990.

MacIntyre, Ferren. "ENSO, Climate Variability, and the Rapanui, Part II. Oceanography and Rapa Nui." *Rapa Nui Journal* 15, no. 2 (October 2001).

Mann, D., J. Chase, J. Edwards, W. Beck, R. Reanier, and M. Mass. "Prehistoric Destruction of the Primeval Soils and Vegetation of Rapa Nui." In *Easter Island: Scientific Exploration into the World's Environmental Problems in Microcosm,* edited by John Loret and John T. Tanacredi, 133–53. New York: Kluwer Academic, 2003.

Martinsson-Wallin, Helene, and Paul Wallin. "Ahu and Settlement: Archaeological Excavations at Anakena and La Perouse." In *Easter Island Archaeology: Research on Early Rapa Nui Culture,* edited by Christopher M. Stevenson and William S. Ayres, 27–43. Los Osos, CA: Easter Island Foundation, 2000.

Martinsson-Wallin, Helene, and Paul Wallin. "Excavations at Anakena. The Easter Island Settlement Sequence and Change of Subsistence." In *Easter Island and East Polynesian Prehistory, Proceedings of the Second International Congress on Easter Island and East Polynesia,* edited by Patricia Vargas Casanova, 179–86. Santiago: Universidad de Chile, Instituto de Estudios Isla de Pascua, 1998.

———. "The Settlement/Activity Area Nau Nau East at Anakena, Easter Island." In *Archaeological Investigations at Anakena, Easter Island,* edited by Arne Skjølsvold, 122–216. The Kon-Tiki Museum Occasional Papers 3. Oslo: Kon-Tiki Museum, 1994.

Martinsson-Wallin, Helene, and Susan J. Crockford. "Early Settlement of Rapa Nui." *Asian Perspectives* 40, no. 2 (2002): 244–78.

Maude, Henry Evans. *Slavers in Paradise: the Peruvian Labour Trade in Polynesia, 1862–1864.* Stanford, CA: Stanford University Press, 1981.

McCoy, Patrick. "Easter Island." In *The Prehistory of Polynesia,* edited by Jesse D. Jennings, 135–66. Cambridge, MA: Harvard University Press, 1979.

McCoy, Patrick. *Easter Island Settlement Patterns in the Late Prehistoric and Protohistoric Periods.* PhD dissertation. Washington State University, 1973.

McCoy, Patrick. "Excavation of a Rectangular House on

the East Rim of Rano Kau Volcano, Easter Island." *Archaeology and Physical Anthropology in Oceania* 8 (1973): 51–57.

Mellén Blanco, Francisco. *Manuscritos y documentos españoles para la historia de la Isla de Pascua: La expedición del Capitán D. Felipe González de Haedo a la Isla de David.* Madrid, Spain: El Centro de Estudios Históricos de Obras Públicas y Urbanismo (CEHOPU) Biblioteca, 1986.

Métraux, Alfred. *Ethnology of Easter Island.* Bernice P. Bishop Museum Bulletin 160. Honolulu: Bernice P. Bishop Museum, 1971.

Mieth, Andreas, Hans-Rudolf Bork, and Ingo Feeser. "Prehistoric and Recent Land Use Effects on Poike Peninsula, Easter Island (Rapa Nui)." *Rapa Nai Journal* 16, no. 2 (2002): 89–95.

Mulloy, William. "The Ceremonial Center of Vinapu." In *Archaeology of Easter Island: Reports of the Norwegian Archaeological Expedition to Easter Island and the East Pacific*, vol. 1, edited by Thor Heyerdahl and Edwin Ferdon Jr., 93–180. School of American Research and the Museum of New Mexico Monograph 24. Stockholm: Forum Publishing House, 1961.

———. "A Preliminary Culture-Historical Research Model for Easter Island." In *Las Islas Oceánicas de Chile*, vol. 1, edited by Gloria Echeverria Duco and Patricio Arana Espina, 105–51. Santiago: Universidad de Chile, Instituto de Estudios Internacionales, 1979.

———. *Preliminary Report of Archaeological Field Work February–July 1968, Easter Island.* Bulletin 1. New York: Easter Island Committee, International Fund for Monuments, 1968.

———. *Preliminary Report of the Restoration of Ahu Vai Uri, Easter Island.* Bulletin 2. New York: Easter Island Committee, International Fund for Monuments, 1970.

———. "A Speculative Reconstruction of Techniques of Carving, Transporting and Erecting Easter Island Statues." *Archaeology and Physical Anthropology in Oceania* 1 (1970): 1–23.

Mulloy, William, and Gonzalo Figueroa. "The A Kivi-Vai Teka Complex and Its Relationship to Easter Island Architectural Prehistory." *Honolulu: Asian and Pacific Archaeology Series* 8 (1978): 131–38.

———. "The Archaeological Heritage of Rapa Nui." Paper presented at Sección de Monumentos y Museos, UNESCO, Paris, June 1966.

NOVA online. *Secrets of Easter Island: Move a Megalith.* http://www.pbs.org/wgbh/nova/easter/move.

Orefici, Giuseppe, Claudio Cristino, Giancarlo Ligabue, Patricia Vargas Casanova, et al. *Proyecto Hanga O Teo, Misión Arqueológica Chileno-Italiana a Isla de Pascua.* Centro Studie Ricerche Ligabue de Venezia, Centro Italiano Studi e Ricerche Archeologiche Precolombiane de Brescia, Instituto de Estudios Isla de Pascua, FAU, Universidad de Chile y Museo Sebastián Englert, Isla de Pascua, 1992.

Orliac, Catherine. "Données Nouvelles sur la Composition de la Flore de Ile des Pâques." *Journal de la Société des Oceanistes* 2 (1998).

———. "The Woody Vegetation of Easter Island Between the Early 14th and the Mid-17th centuries AD." In *Easter Island Archaeology Research on Early Rapa Nui Culture*, edited by Christopher M. Stevenson and William S. Ayres. Los Osos, CA: Easter Foundation, 2000.

Orliac, Catherine, and Michel Orliac. "The Disappearance of Easter Island's Forest: Over-Exploitation or Climatic Catastrophe?" In *Easter Island in Pacific Context, Proceedings of the Fourth International Conference on Easter Island and East Polynesia*, edited by Christopher M. Stevenson, Georgia Lee, and F. J. Morin. Los Osos, CA: Easter Island Foundation, 1998.

———. "Evolution du couvert vegétal á l'Ile de Pâques du 15é au 19é siécle." *Easter Island and East Polynesian Prehistory, Proceedings of the Second International Congress on Easter Island and East Polynesia*, edited by Patricia Vargas Casanova, Capítulo 16. Santiago: Universidad de Chile, Instituto de Estudios Isla de Pascua, 1998.

Orliac, Catherine, Michel Orliac et al. "Arbres et arbustes de l'Ile de Pâques. Composition et évolution de la flore depuis l'arrivée des Polynésien." Rapport Intermediare Mission Archeologique à l'ile de Pâques, Oct.–Nov., 1995.

Pavel, Pavel. "Reconstruction of the Transport of Moai." *State and Perspectives of Scientific Research in Easter Island Culture*, edited by Heide-Margaret Esen-Baur, 141–44. Frankfurt: Courier Forschungsinstitut Senckenberg, 1990.

Roggeveen, Jacob. "Extract from the official log of the voyage of Mynheer Jacob Roggeveen, in the Ships Den Arend Thienhoven and De Afrkaanishe Galey, in 1721–22, in so far as it relates to the discovery of Easter Island." 2nd series, no.13. Cambridge: Hakluyt Society, 1908.

Rolett, Barry. "Turtles, Priests and the Afterworld: A Study in the Iconographic Interpretation of Polynesian Petroglyphs." In *Island Societies*, edited by Patrick V. Kirch. London: Cambridge University Press, 1986.

Isla de Pascua; Estructuras Religioso-ceremoniales en los Cuadrángulos 21, 30, 31, 32 y 33." Manuscripts on file with author, written 1987–1989.

———. "Rapa Nui Settlement Patterns: Types, Function and Spatial Distribution of Households Structural Components." In *Easter Island and East Polynesian Prehistory: Proceedings of the Second International Congress on Easter Island and East Polynesian Archaeology*, edited by Patricia Vargas Casanova, 111–30. Santiago: Universidad de Chile, Instituto de Estudios Isla de Pascua, 1998.

Vargas Casanova, Patricia, ed. *Isla de Pascua: El asentamiento interior de altura; Prospección arqueológica de la vertiente oriental del Maunga Terevaka*. Santiago: University of Chile, Instituto de Estudios Isla de Pascua, FONDECYT, 1989.

Vargas Casanova, Patricia, and Claudio Cristino. "Desarrollo y Proyecciones del Inventario Arqueológico de Isla de Pascua." In *Informe anual a la gobernación provincial Isla de Pascua e Intendencia V Región*. Valparaiso: University of Chile, 1977.

———. Inventario y Prospección Arqueológica de Isla de Pascua, Informe a la Rectoría de la Universidad de Chile. Santiago, Chile, 1978.

———. "La Prospección Arqueológica de Isla de Pascua." Paper presented at the VII Congreso Internacional de Arqueología de Chile, Altos de Vilches, Talca, Chile, 1977.

———. Resultados del Inventario Arqueológico de Isla de Pascua, Informe anual a Conadip/Odeplan. Santiago, Chile, 1977.

Vargas Casanova, Patricia, and José Vinagre. *Caracterización Geográfica de la Vertiente Sur Oriental del Maunga Terevaka*. Serie Documentos de Trabajo: Estudios del Asentamiento, Año VIII. Santiago: Instituto de Estudios Isla de Pascua, 1988.

Vargas Casanova, Patricia, et al. *Prospección Arqueológica en la Península del Poike: Cuadrángulos 24-Vai A Heva y 25-Ana O Keke*. Serie Documentos de Trabajo: Estudios del Asentamiento, Año IX, No. 1. Santiago, Chile, 1989.

Vargas Casanova, Patricia, Claudio Cristino, and Edmundo Edwards. "Moai Arcaicos de Isla de Pascua." Paper presented at the VII Congreso Internacional de Arqueología de Chile, Altos de Vilches, Talca, Chile, 1977.

Vargas Casanova, Patricia, Claudio Cristino, and Roberto Izaurieta. *1000 años en Rapa Nui: Arqueología del asentamiento*. Santiago: Editorial Universitaria, 2006.

———. *Easter Island Archaeological Survey: Quadrangle 31; Ahu Raai, Section Hanga Hoonu*. Serie Documentos de Trabajo: Estudios del Asentamiento III. Santiago, Chile, 1983.

———. "Easter Island Statuary Project Thematic Map: Distribution, Location and Material of 818 Statues Recorded Between 1977–87." In *Archaeology: Proceedings of the First International Congress on Easter Island and East Polynesia, Hanga Roa, Easter Island*, vol. 1, edited by Claudio Cristino et al., 141. Santiago: Universidad de Chile, Instituto de Estudios Isla de Pascua, 1988.

Vargas Casanova, Patricia, Reginald Budd, L. González, and José Vinagre. *Prospección Arqueológica en el Faldeo Sur del Maunga Tere Vaka. Un estudio integral del doblamiento interior en altura.*. Santiago: FONDECYT, 1988.

Vargas Casanova, Patricia, Reginald Budd, Roberto Izaurieta, Claudio Cristino, et al. *Isla de Pascua: Bases para la Formulación de un Programa de Desarrollo. Arqueología, Antropología y Urbanismo*. Santiago: Universidad de Chile, Instituto de Estudios Isla de Pascua, 1990.

Vargas Casanova, Patricia, Claudio Cristino, Roberto Izaurieta, et al. *Prospección arqueológica en la costa norte de Isla de Pascua: Area entre Taharoa y Hanga O Puna hasta la Vertiente Norte del Rano Raraku; Secciones de los Cuadrángulos No. 20-Ahu O Pepe; No. 21-Mahatua y No. 31-Ahu Raai*. Santiago, Chile, 1991.

———. *Prospección arqueológica: Un estudio integral, básico para la planificación y desarrollo de Isla de Pascua; Diagnóstico, evaluación y proyecciones del recurso cultural*. Santiago: Universidad de Chile, Instituto de Estudios Isla de Pascua, FONDECYT, 1989.

Vargas Casanova, Patricia, Roberto Izaurieta, Claudio Cristino, and Carlos Arias. "New Approaches to Settlement Patterns Studies of the Easter Island Archaeological Survey Data." In *Easter Island and East Polynesian Prehistory: Proceedings of the Second International Congress on Easter Island and East Polynesian Archaeology*, edited by Patricia Vargas Casanova, 147–52. Santiago: Universidad de Chile, Instituto de Estudios Isla de Pascua, 1998.

Vargas Casanova, Patricia, Roberto Izaurieta, Claudio Cristino, et al. *Estudios del asentamiento:Prospección y excavaciones arqueológicas de sitios habitacionales*. Serie Documentos de Trabajo: Estudios del Asentamiento, Año XII, No. 2. Institutio de Estudios Isla de Pascua. Santiago, Chile, 1992.

———. *Investigaciones arqueológicas en la localidad de Akahanga. Cuadrángulo 7, Sitio 7–553*. Santiago: Institutio de Estudios Isla de Pascua, 1993.

Vargas Casanova, Patricia, Roberto Izaurieta, Reginald Budd, et al. *Estudios del asentamiento de Isla de Pascua: Prospección arqueológica de la península del Poike y sector de Mahatua*. Santiago: Universidad de Chile, 1990.

Weisler, Marshall I. "Hard Evidence for Prehistoric Interaction in Polynesia." *Current Anthropology* 39 (1998): 521–32.

———. "Issues in the Colonization and Settlement of Polynesian Islands." In *Easter Island and East Polynesian Prehistory*, edited by Patricia Vargas Casanova, 73–86. Santiago: Universidad de Chile, Instituto de Estudios Isla de Pascua, 1998.

Weisler, Marshall I., and Roger C. Green. "The Many Sides of Polynesian Archaeology in Reference to the Colonization Process in Southwest Polynesia." *Rapa Nui Journal* 22, no. 2 (2008): 85–86.

Yen, Douglas. "Easter Island Agriculture in Prehistory. The Possibilities of Reconstruction." *Archaeology: First International Congress Easter Island and East Polynesia*, edited by Claudio Cristino, Patricia Vargas Casanova, Roberto Izaurieta, and Reginald Budd. Santiago: Universidad de Chile, Instituto de Estudios Isla de Pascua, 1988.

———. "The Sweet Potato and Oceania." Bernice P. Bishop Museum Bulletin 236. Honolulu: Bernice P. Bishop Museum, 1974.

INDEX

Page numbers in italics indicate illustrations.

CONTRIBUTORS

Kenneth Treister, FAIA, architect, artist, photographer, and author, received the Silver Metal and Lifetime Achievement Award from the AIA Miami. In 2013, he was awarded the Gold Medal by the AIA Florida, its highest honor. He has lectured at universities in the United States, Chile, China, Israel, Indonesia, India, Malaysia, and Bali and was adjunct professor of architecture at both the University of Miami and the University of Florida. He has been published in over fifty professional journals, and he has written nine books, including his most recent, *Havana Forever: A Pictorial and Cultural History of an Unforgettable City* and *Maya Architecture: Temples in the Sky*. He produced four documentaries on architecture, including *Silent Sentinels: The Mystery of Easter Island* (1990). Treister also sculpted Miami Beach's world famous, soul-wrenching masterpiece, The Holocaust Memorial.

Studying Easter Island has been the life's work of archaeologists **Patricia Vargas Casanova** and **Claudio Cristino**. They moved to Easter Island in 1976 for the restoration of the birdman cult site of Orongo. In 1979, they founded the Easter Island Studies Centre at the University of Chile, now the Easter Island and Oceania Studies Centre. In 1977, they began the Easter Island Archaeological Survey that has recorded over 20,000 archaeological sites; the mapping of almost 900 moai; the quarries of Rano Raraku (1981); and the restoration of the Ahu Tongariki monument.

Vargas Casanova is a full professor and Cristino an associate professor at the University of Chile, and both are principals at the Pacific Islands Research and Education Institute (PIRI) and the Eastern Pacific Research Foundation (EPRF). They also direct the University of Chile's Institute for Easter Island Studies. In 2011, the Explorers Club awarded them the prestigious Lowell Thomas Award as distinguished explorers.